Praise for Al

"Alan Cohen is a major, major playe~
world. He is one of my favorite authors, and I want powerful,
enlightened, conscious people to read and APPLY his messages."

—Dr. Wayne W. Dyer, author of *The Power of Intention*

"No one in my life has contributed more to my movement down the
path of expanded consciousness and greater awareness than Alan
Cohen."

—Neale Donald Walsch, author of *Conversations with God*

"Alan Cohen is the most eloquent spokesman of the heart."

—James Redfield, author of *The Celestine Prophecy*

"Alan Cohen is a teacher of great warmth and wit with a marvelous
gift for storytelling."

—Dr. Joan Borysenko, author of *Fire In the Soul*

"The way Alan Cohen shares his heart in books and tapes is a positive and dynamic force, making significant contributions to healing
humanity."

—Dr. Jerry Jampolsky, author of *Love Is Letting Go of Fear*

"As a teacher, Alan Cohen has a rare and precious quality. He
inspires happiness, and the message itself is as pure as his heart."

—Hugh Prather, author of *Notes to Myself*

"Alan Cohen is one of the most gentle and powerful guiding lights
of the profound transition now occurring on earth."

—Barbara Marx Hubbard, author of *The Hunger of Eve*

Praise for Alan Cohen

About the Author

—〰—

Alan Cohen is the author of many popular inspirational books, including *The Dragon Doesn't Live Here Anymore*, the award-winning *A Deep Breath of Life*, and the popular *Why Your Life Sucks and What You Can Do About It*. He is a contributing writer for the *New York Times* #1 best-selling series *Chicken Soup for the Soul*, and his books have been translated into twenty-one foreign languages. A frequent guest on television and radio, he conducts life mastery seminars in Hawaii and on-line, and is an acclaimed keynote speaker for educational, health, church, and corporate groups. He lives with his family on Maui, Hawaii.

Also by Alan Cohen:

Are You as Happy as Your Dog?
Dare to Be Yourself
A Deep Breath of Life
The Dragon Doesn't Live Here Anymore
Handle with Prayer
Happily Even After
Have You Hugged a Monster Today?
I Had It All the Time
Joy is my Compass
Lifestyles of the Rich in Spirit
Looking in for Number One
Mr. Everit's Secret
My Father's Voice
The Peace that You Seek
Relax into Wealth
Rising in Love
Setting the Seen
Why Your Life Sucks and What You Can Do about It
Wisdom of the Heart

DON'T GET LUCKY, GET SMART

Why Your Love Life Sucks—
and What You Can Do about It

Alan Cohen

MARLOWE & COMPANY
NEW YORK

To all my relations:
Every woman, man, family member, and friend
who has been a valued learning partner
on my journey into love

Don't Get Lucky, Get Smart:
Why Your Love Life Sucks—and What You Can Do about It

Copyright © 2007 Alan Cohen Publications Inc.

Published by
Marlowe & Company
11 Cambridge Center
Cambridge, MA 02142

AVALON
publishing group incorporated

Library of Congress Cataloging-in-Publication Data

Cohen, Alan, 1950-
  Don't get lucky-get smart : why your love life sucks-and what you can do about it
/ Alan Cohen.
    p. cm.
  Includes bibliographical references.
  ISBN-13: 978-1-60094-059-0
  ISBN-10: 1-60094-059-5
  1. Man-woman relationships. 2. Mate selection. 3. Love. I. Title.
HQ801.C626 2007
646.7'7--dc22

                                    2007018667

        9 8 7 6 5 4 3 2
    Interior design by Maria E. Torres
    Printed in the United States of America

Contents

Introduction

—∿—

WHY DO SO MANY relationships start with fireworks and end in the pits? Why do connections that open your heart ultimately break it? Why would Rita Rudner confess, "Whenever I date a guy, I think, 'Is this the man I want my children to spend their weekends with?'"

Let's face it: the dating game is fraught with pitfalls and minefields. Unless you really know what you're doing, you can get balled up, walled up, and dismally frustrated. In your quest for Mr. or Ms. Right, you are likely to encounter a motley parade of strange rangers; round and round you go, ferreting through online match services, singles bars, parties, support groups, psychics, and setups by (soon-to-be-former) friends, searching for The One I Have Waited for My Whole Life, or at least Someone I Can Get Along with for More Than a Month. You start to wonder if there's anyone out there who is available and you actually *like*.

I am qualified to teach about dating hell because I trudged through it for many years—until the flames decimated the illusions that kept me captive. Over time, through trial and error (mostly error) I found my way out and mapped the terrain along the way. Now I am passing my notes along to you, along with those of others whose pains and triumphs have led them to great connections they once believed impossible. There *is* a path out of the Disenchanted Forest, and you may be closer to it than you know.

In the pages that follow you will meet people like yourself: People just trying to hook up with someone who can carry on a conversation longer than "Yo." People who found themselves in scary, confusing, and distasteful situations and wondered if there was more to relationships than fighting, drama, head games, and gradually diminishing sex. People who had a huge disappointment or many little ones. People trying to find the handle to the door out of a room they weren't quite sure how they got into. You will also meet people who finally stepped into their power, tapped into their true deservingness, and found someone who made the journey worth it. Their insights will become your own, and as you apply them, your path will become lighter, faster, and easier.

Each chapter opens with a true account from my own experience or from that of my seminar and coaching clients, individuals or couples trying to have a rewarding date or relationship. You will see the mistakes they made and how they got it together—or didn't. No matter how they ended up, you will grow with them. Their story, you will realize, is your story. And how will your story end? If you apply the "What You Can Do About It" keys you find here, you will experience unprecedented progress in your love life and pen your own desired script.

Some of the themes and reasons may jump out at you as applying especially to you, and you will find suggestions that will help you specifically. Do read all of the chapters, as you may be surprised to find that many of the insights apply to people you are dating and can help you understand why they do what they do, why you are attracted to them, and how to correct patterns that aren't working. *All* of the material here can help guide you out of dating hell.

No matter how many dating fiascos and relationship hurricanes you have weathered, there is hope. Your forays to dating hell have not been a curse or punishment; instead, think of them as field trips to gather data. They have helped you to discover what you want, to recognize that you deserve it, and to gain the courage and confidence to ask for it. Every date and relationship, no matter how weird or wonderful, has brought you to the place where you now stand. If you want better, you can have it. But like any craftsperson, you need good tools. Practicing the principles in this book will accelerate your progress tremendously and save you lots of trials and errors. So let's turn down the flames and turn up the light.

—Alan Cohen

Some notes for the reader:

—◦◦◦—

1. All the anecdotal stories noted at the beginning of each chapter are true. In many, names have been changed to honor the privacy of the person or couple described. For the sake of brevity and illustration, some of the stories are composites of several different individuals or couples who have had a similar experience.

2. Most of the couples described here are heterosexual couples. If you are a gay or lesbian reader, you can apply these principles equally powerfully to your relationship(s). Although I understand that you might face issues that are unique to gay and lesbian relationships, I will defer to others who are more expert in those areas than me, and concentrate here on issues that are useful for anyone seeking to find fulfillment with a partner, regardless of gender.

3. Use your personal discretion in applying the suggestions, exercises, and practices you find here. Some may be more appropriate for you than others. I suggest you consult your inner guidance as to what will be helpful for you. I further suggest that you discuss any significant actions or life changes with a qualified counselor, coach, or therapist.

REASON #1.

YOU START RELATIONSHIPS ON THE WRONG FOOT.

How and why you start a relationship makes a huge difference in how it turns out. Choosing the wrong person or getting involved for the wrong reasons will offset your efforts and land you back where you started, more frustrated than ever. If you keep meeting partners who disappoint you, it may be time to examine how and why you get involved and upgrade your choices so that you choose people who will join you where you want to go.

WHAT YOU CAN DO ABOUT IT

The following chapters will show you how to:
- Navigate when you fall in love.
- Recognize red flags of potentially problematic partners.
- Move from desperation to self-confidence.
- Attract a partner by being your authentic self.
- Build relationships on intimacy, not fantasy.

Love at First Sight?

———

When Steve met Debbie at a party, it was love at first sight. Both instantly knew they were soul mates, had sex soon and often, proclaimed their true love to each other, and announced themselves as an item to their friends.

After a few months Debbie moved in with Steve, and the couple enjoyed a honeymoon period. Before long, however, they began to notice things about each other they did not like. At first these were little things, like Steve leaving the toilet seat up and Debbie needing to have the bedroom shades closed so that the sun would not wake her too early in the morning.

The couple's upsets intensified when they discovered each other's habits. Steve watched football most of the weekend and did not much care to talk about his feelings. Debbie wanted to discuss their relationship and began to pressure Steve for a commitment.

Over time, Steve and Debbie began to fight more than they were enjoying each other. Privately they each shook their heads and wondered, "What happened to that wonderful person I met?" Steve complained, "She has lots of insecurities I didn't see." Debbie decided, "Something in him changed when we moved in together."

Eventually the couple's issues became so heated that Debbie moved out. At first the two tried to be friends and date, but their time together reverted to the same arguments they had had while living together. Then they just stopped seeing each other and felt resentful about love at first sight having gone sour.

Does this story sound familiar? Did I read your diary? Did you just read mine?

Sometimes love at first sight is really that. People meet, recognize each other as soul mates, fall in love, and live happy lives together. Amen.

More often, however, love at first sight is hope at first sight. Or intense yearning for a mate at first sight. Or hot sex at first sight. Or rebound from a painful breakup at first sight. Or all kinds of other stuff at first sight. Yet there is one way to tell if the attraction really is love at first sight: If you stay together over time and grow happier in each other's company, it was. If you don't, it wasn't.

If your relationship stands the test of upright toilet seats and downright shades; fears, mistrust, jealousy, and incongruent sexual rhythms; how much to spend and how much to save; which relatives to invite for Christmas and which to avoid; and all the other issues that crop up in a relationship—it truly was love at first sight. If any or all of those issues blow you out of the water, it wasn't quite love at first sight. Or if it was, your fear and resistance overshadowed the love.

Although we have been taught that if you can just find the right person, all will be well, there is more to it that. Dating and relationship are less about finding someone who can make you happy, and more about finding where your own happiness lives. It would be easier to have a white knight or ravishing maiden sweep you off your feet, but until then you might want to take another look in the mirror. What you seek may be closer than you know.

WHAT TO DO IF IT HAPPENS TO YOU

If you should fall in love at first sight, enjoy it. Love is the greatest rush in the world; it's how we were born to feel and live. Suddenly the humdrum routine of your life morphs to vibrant color, major life issues shrink to petty nothings, and the whole world is bright and new. Now the long journey you took to get to this place seems worthwhile. Even people you didn't like are somehow tolerable, and you don't even mind going home and dealing with your family at Thanksgiving. Thank God for true love! Without it the planet is a dull and dreary place; with it life has beauty, meaning, and purpose.

Now for the fine print:

Breathe. Take it step-by-step. Get to know your partner before you make any major decisions. Let the love prove itself. If it's good, it will last, and you will be happy. If it's not real, you don't want it.

That's the relative size of these ideas when you are swimming in a sea of heady love. You can hardly read them, because you are having such a good time—and who wants to study the details? You are in love!

Now please expand these words in your mind to a very large font size:

Breathe. Take it step-by-step. Get to know your partner before you make any major decisions. Let the love prove itself. If it's good, it will last, and you will be happy. If it's not real, you don't want it.

Okay, I made my point. Funny thing is, for some people this type size will still be unreadable—make that *invisible*. If I printed these words big enough to flash on the huge monitor atop Times Square, they would still not be legible to some people. Why not? Because "a man hears what he wants to hear and disregards the rest." Yet if this advice saves you a trip to the twenty-four-hour Chapel of Elvis in Las Vegas, needless heartache, or strife with your partner, it is well worth noting. Before discussing names for your children, be sure you know your partner's.

ARE YOU A SERIAL ROMANTIC?

Many people who fall in love at first sight do so regularly. I used to meet my soul mate at least once a month (more often in summer). I met a woman who did the same. We dated for a while, but broke up because we were so addicted to seeking that we didn't know how to handle finding. We were masters of romance, but fledglings at relationship. She later married a man who swept her off her feet by taking her to Paris for a romantic weekend. Later, on their way to their Tahitian honeymoon, the couple started arguing on the airplane, and by the time the honeymoon was over, so was the marriage. I could have tattooed the above big-font advice on the inside of her contact lenses, and she still wouldn't have seen it.

Yet serial romance serves a purpose. With every new chapter you learn more about who you are, what you want, and how to master having a relationship. Sometimes we benefit more from short-lived, fiery, or painful relationships than from long, boring ones. If you have had lots of relationships and wonder if you will ever find (or be) the right person, take heart. Every date and relationship brings you closer to having what you want. One day—maybe sooner than you know—the wisdom you have accumulated will reach the tipping point, and your learning curve will pay off. Just don't lurch at someone because he says his favorite movie is *Sleepless in Seattle*. Developing your relationship with yourself may be more productive in the long run.

In real love you want the other
person's good. In romantic love,
you want the other person.
—Margaret Anderson

If you tend to fall in love on a regular basis, take the best and leave the rest. Notice what you do that keeps your heart open and what you do that shuts it down. You don't have to fall in love to be in love. You can rise in love. When you fall in love, you give your power away to your partner. When you rise in love, you maintain your wholeness. If you fall in love easily, you fall out of it just as easily. When you recognize that you (not another person) are the source of your loving, you can stay in love—maybe not every moment, but enough to a make the journey worthwhile.

My friend Tom realized it was time for him to create one good lasting relationship when he couldn't keep track of his various dates' family issues. He knew that one woman's father was a control freak; another's brother was in a mental institution; another was in love with her stepmother's nephew; and another left home when her Quaalude-addicted father began slurring his sentences like Ozzy Osbourne. For the life of him, he couldn't remember which dysfunctional drama belonged to whom. Tom considered buying a Palm Pilot to catalog the assorted neuroses and avoid the embarrassment of asking the Ozzy defector about her nutty brother, which could have caused more of a rift than calling out the wrong name in bed. Ultimately Tom decided it would be a lot easier to remember just one set of weird relations than many, and he swears his life is easier for it.

GROW YOUR LOVE WITH INTIMACY

I know some couples who fell in love immediately and went on to have great relationships and marriages; they are inspiring but cluster in the short end of the bell curve. I know others who got together quickly, fought like hell, and duked it out until they learned to harmonize. Other couples met, got to know and like each other, grew in love over time, and went on to have great relationships and marriages. There are lots of ways to get to the same place. The important thing to remember is that all of this doesn't just happen to you randomly. Your thoughts, feelings, attitudes, expectations, and sense of inner worth are far more determining factors than chance. "Getting lucky" may refer to unexpected good sex or meeting someone fantastic out of the blue, but it has little to do with building a quality relationship. The principles that guide true love, like all of life, are consistent, reliable, and completely within your power to employ on your behalf by conscious choice. Depending on getting lucky to meet your soul mate is like depending on winning the lottery to finance your home. It could happen, but I wouldn't count on it. You don't need to get lucky to have a great relationship. You just need to get smart.

One of the surest ways to build a solid relationship is to let your passion grow with intimacy rather than trying to catch intimacy up to romance. Although the symbols of intimacy are tantalizingly attractive—spending days and nights together exclusively, candlelit dinners, sunset walks on the beach, moving in together—they may be empty of the substance that will give your relationship legs. Let the symbols of romance proceed from true connection, rather than trying to wedge the connection in the cracks between the symbols.

The more you show your partner your real self, your passions, your visions, your fears and deepest feelings, the closer you will become. There are five levels of communication through which most people relate, each of which bears reward according to the depth of personal investment behind it:

1. *News, weather, gossip, politics, sports, and public infor-mation.* The stuff you talk about with taxi drivers, neighbors, and coworkers at the water cooler: "Hot enough for you, Carl?" "Hey, what about those 49ers?" "Did you hear that Tom and Suzy broke up?" Small talk, common-ground conversation with little or no personal investment. Appropriate here and there, helps to create some connection with people you might otherwise not relate to, but rela-tively devoid of substance.

2. *Stories.* How you met your husband; the time you scored the winning touchdown; the funny thing Garrett said to his teacher. May or may not reveal elements of yourself. If you repeat the same story time and again, you are hiding behind it and prob-ably boring your listener. If you bring honesty, pas-sion, and aliveness to it, you are signaling your partner to meet you there.

3. *Your opinions and judgments:* "Your flyer was attrac-tive, but I think it would look better with some more pictures." "Jerry will value his car more if he earns the money to buy it than if we just buy it for him." "I wish they would give more Oscars to independent films." Reveals more of yourself and invites the lis-tener to respond with more of him- or herself.

4. *Your feelings:* "I'm really nervous about Cindy going off to college." "I hate my job and wish I didn't have to go to work." "I feel so attracted to Carol, but I get tongue-tied when I'm around her." Shares more intimate aspects of yourself, creating a stronger platform for intimacy.

5. *Your most intimate and vulnerable feelings:* "I feel closer to you than anyone I have ever been with." "I'm afraid I made a big mistake moving in with you so quickly." "I deeply want to quit my job, but I don't know how I will support my kids." Puts your heart on the line, showing pieces of you that you are tender and deeply personal. Such feelings are not appropriate to share with people you may not know or trust, but can take you to deeply rewarding places with a trustworthy partner and build a relationship on your real selves.

The more of yourself you reveal, the more you risk—but not really. If someone rejects you because they see the real you and don't want it, you are better off letting them go. Someone else will be thrilled to be with you just as you are, and they are the prize worth seeking and waiting for.

A BIZARRE ANCIENT RITUAL

In olden times, people would practice a strange ritual called courting. (You can probably find some historical information about it on the Internet.) If a young man was interested in a young lady, he would go to her house and the two would sit on a swing on the porch and talk for a while. A few nights later he might take her out for a soda and maybe hold her hand on the way home. The next week they would go to a movie. They just kept doing stuff together and hopefully liking each other more, which eventually led to hot, sweaty, no-holds-barred, swinging from the rafters, screaming-to-wake-up-the neighbors sex. (I just wanted to keep you motivated.) Weird and old-fashioned as it may sound, there may be some value in getting to know someone before committing your life to him or her.

If you fall in love with someone at first sight, you obviously have chemistry. You are better off than couples who do not have chemistry and try in vain to manufacture it. So you are off to a good start. Just keep the flame burning by building your relationship rather than hoping it will save you. Then you can cook for a long time without getting singed, and, who knows, maybe even like each other. Then you will build your relationship by choice, not chance. You will have a meaningful partner with whom you can grow and deepen over time, and your relationship will only get better, because you got to know each other as real people, not fantasies. And you won't need to get lucky, because you created good fortune rather than waiting for it to smile on you.

WHAT YOU CAN DO ABOUT IT, POINT BY POINT

- Enjoy the great feelings of love at first sight and appreciate meeting a person who might be a great partner.
- Be aware that what feels like love at first sight may be hope, fantasy, rebound, or sex at first sight.

- Take your time, get to know your partner, and let the relationship reveal itself. If it's good, it will last.
- Do not make major commitments or life changes until you have more experience with your partner. Let your decisions unfold in their own right timing.
- Develop intimacy by sharing your most valued ideas, feelings, experiences, and visions with your partner, and inviting him or her to do the same. Get to know each other from the inside out.

Realness Rocks

—∾—

When I was growing up, my parents did not reward me for telling the truth, but for saying what they wanted to hear. When I began to have relationships with women, I was astute enough to figure out and say what was pleasing, carefully avoiding comments that might upset them. Those relationships did not have a lot of depth or longevity.

Then one day in the heat of an argument with a girlfriend, she exhorted me, "Just tell me what you are really thinking and feeling! It may knock me down, but I'll get up again. If you don't show me who you are, I have no idea what's going on and I can't relate to you at all."

Her message got to me. For the first time I believed that a woman actually wanted to hear what was going on inside me more than words that would meet her expectations. That realization set off a revolutionary shift in my relationships. Since that time I have attracted relationships based on truth more than charade, and in the process I have found far richer depth and wholeness. While this journey has required vigilance and has sometimes been uncomfortable, it is far more rewarding than trying to be someone I am not.

In the film *Cross My Heart*, David and Kathy wreck their first date by lying about who they are. David has just lost his job, but he wants to impress Kathy, so he tells her he has just received a promotion. Then he borrows his playboy buddy's slick sports car and arranges to use his swanky pad for the evening.

Kathy has her own secrets: she has a young daughter and she smokes. Worried that David will lose interest in her if he discovers these dating debits, she does not introduce David to her daughter and she sneaks smokes at every opportunity.

The couple plunges into a convoluted escapade, less about getting to know each other and more about protecting facades. For every fib Kathy and David tell, they have to weave three more to uphold it. Eventually the date deteriorates into a disastrous comedy of concealment.

By the end of the evening the fibs hit the fan and both are exposed. Busted, Kathy and David sheepishly admit their fears and reasons for deception—their first honest communication. Buoyed by this moment of truth, they decide to try another date, this time as their real selves.

Finally we see David pulling up to Kathy's house in his funky little beater car. Kathy answers with a cigarette in hand and calls her daughter to meet her date. Ah, the breath of truth. David and Kathy aren't perfect, but at least they are real. Now they stand a chance.

As soon as you trust yourself,
you will know how to live.
—Goethe

Dating and relationships work only when both partners are authentic. Hiding, withholding, or game playing will undermine your efforts and keep you from the connection you seek. The sad irony of deceptive relationships is that the truth you fear would blow your relationship apart is often the very element that would bring you closer together. When you value honesty more than presentation, you have a real shot at dates and relationships that work.

FROM IMAGE MANAGEMENT TO REALNESS

One dating tip cuts through many superficial ones: *Show up as yourself.* The more you seek to impress, the more you will need to impress. Rather than sweating to manage your image, manage your fear and insecure thoughts that tell you that you have to get people to like you. The harder you try to prove yourself, the dorkier you come across. People who do not need to please are irresistible, because they radiate wholeness, a rare delicacy in a world of hungry hearts.

Image Managers	Real Players
Posture to attract and impress	Trust self to be enough
Focus on physical presentation	Focus on mind, feelings, spirit
Use stock lines and stories	Are spontaneously honest
Equate a quality date with money spent	Equate quality with connection
Drop names and photos	Need no accolades
Are goal-oriented in dates (sex, money, ring)	Enjoy each moment as it comes
Seek approval	Are confident in self and process
Are easily offended or insulted	Take upsets in stride

You will attract a partner who matches you when you offer your true self to match. Presenting a diluted version of yourself will result in your receiving diluted versions of others. People need to *look* cool only when they don't realize they *are* cool. So your best bet is to discover and bring forth the part of you that *is* cool—the real you—and let that essence attract people who recognize it. This may sound like a big risk in a world of phonies, but trust me, there are some wonderful people out there.

The more you respect yourself, the greater your power to connect with others who do the same. Let your clothes, car, home, and friendship choices express who you are rather than who you are trying to be. Wear Gucci because *you* like it, not because you hope someone else will. Then you will meet someone who is attracted to you more than your clothes, and will never wonder if he will still love you if you wear different jeans.

You will never *become* someone, because you already *are* someone. The greatest achievement of your life is to become who you already are. Then your presence will be absolutely compelling. Heads will turn wherever you walk, because most people are aching to reclaim their lost selves, and when they see someone who walks in confidence, a part of them quickens and wants more of it. So dump your lines, games, hooks, and excuses, and apply generous quantities of realness. Then watch your love life skyrocket, fueled by realness, the most potent aphrodisiac.

HOW TO ATTRACT A REAL PARTNER OR TRANSFORM A PHONY ONE

If you are dating someone who spends a lot time hustling to impress, you must establish realness as the platform of your connection. You might:

1. Lovingly tell your partner that you value her more for who she is than who she is trying to be.
2. Compliment and praise him when he reveals any aspect of his true self.
3. Call her on her stuff when she does something overtly phony.
4. Tell him that authenticity is so important to you that you can't imagine being in a relationship without it.
5. Be so real yourself that she is compelled to meet you there.

Speak, through your words and actions, to the person who wants to be authentic, not the one who believes he or she needs to prove something. You have the power to call forth the best in your partner by seeing and treating him as who he is at his best.

Ultimately your strongest tool to build a real relationship is to be the kind of person you want to attract. Attempts to force a partner to change usually backfire, while living the values you desire have stronger power to lift your partner to where you would like to meet her. When you model realness and invite your partner to do the same, she will either step up or leave. In either case you will be closer to creating a relationship between believable partners.

YOU CAN'T IMPROVE ON PERFECTION

Somewhere along your way someone taught you what you needed to do to become worthy, which undermined your self-confidence. So you set out on a long, lonely, frustrating journey to learn how to dance so other people would like you. But if you do not value yourself, how can you expect someone else to? Rather than adding more requirements to your list of beauty needs, return to who you were before you were told you needed to be other than you are. Then your nakedness will be not a source of shame, but extraordinary empowerment.

Being the best you is not a matter of attainment; it is a matter of bringing forth the best that is already there. While you believe you are on the journey to find your true mate, you are more on a journey to find your true self. Your struggle to get others to like you is a reflection of your struggle to get *you* to like you. Once you do, the game will shift entirely, and you will never need to hide again.

WHAT YOU CAN DO ABOUT IT, POINT BY POINT

- Show up to dates and relationships as yourself, exactly as you are, where you are. Drop any attempts to impress, prove yourself, manipulate, or play games.
- The clearer the signal you put out representing who you are and what you want, the faster and easier the Law of Attraction will join you with someone who matches you.
- If you are with someone who is not acting authentically, encourage him to be more real with you by modeling the realness you seek.
- Attracting the right partner is less about becoming someone you are not, and more about letting go of what you are not.
- The more you like yourself for who you are, the more others will like you for who you are.

Are You Desperate?

―~~―

Sharon is a thirty-eight-year-old advertising executive with a lot going for her. Attractive and savvy, she enjoys a substantial income, a gracious home, and stimulating friends, and has lots of men interested in her. Yet Sharon had an Achilles heel that kept her from connecting with quality men—she felt desperate. Desperate for a man, desperate for a relationship, and desperate to have a child while she still could. Consequently, emotionally unhealthy men would find Sharon and generate dramas that sent her fleeing. To make matters worse, Sharon would get hung up on first dates trying to decide if this man would be a good father to her future children.

In coaching I encouraged Sharon to recognize her beauty, power, and worth to attract a relationship out of choice, not desperation. I also pointed out that her frantic desire to have a child was distracting her from seeing potential partners clearly and growing a relationship naturally.

Over time, Sharon began to recognize her wholeness, and she let go of needing someone to validate her. Before long she met a good man and created a rewarding relationship. Then, as Sharon began to relax and play more, her obsession to immediately have a child dissipated. She realized that her desire for a child was largely influenced by her quest to reclaim her own innocence and playfulness. Sharon might still have a child, but if she does, it (like her relationship) will be because she wants to, not because she has to.

People who feel desperate do desperate things and create desperate results. You are not desperate. Desperation is an interpretation, not a fact. Trace your desperate thoughts and feelings back to their source—a sense of fear, lack, unworthiness, or powerlessness. Then, as you recognize that you are bigger and stronger than these oppressive notions, you will become aware of healthy, viable options you could not see when you were provoked by belief in emptiness.

A DESPERATION INVENTORY

Answering the following questions will help you assess where you stand on the desperation scale:

- Do you go along with distasteful dating choices because you are afraid of what will happen if you don't?
- Do you feel an urgency to find a partner quickly before you get older and less attractive?
- Are you concerned that others will think less of you because you do not have a partner?

- Do you believe that if someone knew the whole truth about you, they would not like or want you?
- Do you go out with people because you do not want to stay home alone?
- Do you put up with physical, emotional, or verbal abuse because you fear that your partner would leave you if you confronted him?
- Do you go from one relationship to another with little or no time in between?
- Are you considering marrying someone because you are afraid no one else will come along?
- Does your desire to have a child blind you to red flags in a relationship?

If you answered "yes" to any of these questions, consider the following: How would you be acting differently if you believed in yourself more? If you knew that you are okay as you are, where you are, what new dating or relationship choices would you make? To whom would you gravitate? Who and what would you let go of? Can you love yourself enough that you don't need someone else to approve of you? What would a confident person do in this situation?

Within you live greater strength and wholeness than you realize. Tap in to these attributes and watch your relationships reflect this power.

TIME TO REALIGN

One of my clients spent a tragicomic weekend with a wealthy man she didn't really like. Marnie agreed to travel to Chicago to be with the fellow, largely because she didn't want to sit home alone. Their time together turned into a sitcom-like fiasco. First Marnie dropped her cell phone in Lake Michigan. Then, as the two were trying to find their way to a certain restaurant, they got lost for forty-five minutes—even though Marnie knew the city very well and had never been lost there before. And on and on.

Afterward, Marnie realized that those strange things happened because she was out of alignment with herself. She had agreed to spend intimate time with someone she didn't care for, and that set up an inner conflict that played itself out in wacky events. People who act in accord with their true choices do not drop cell phones in lakes or get seriously lost. When you are in your right place for the right purpose, events flow easily and successfully. When things start to go steadily wrong, you are receiving signs that you have veered from your path. At such a point your best move is to stop, step back, and be more honest about what your real choices would be. Then you can make new choices that match your true intentions, and generate results that work.

NO ONE CAN COMPLETE YOU

Jerry Maguire's famous line, "You complete me," dealt a nasty blow to people seeking to create a healthy love relationship. No one can complete you, because you are already whole. If someone can complete you, they can uncomplete you and thus open the trapdoor to relationship hell. When you let someone complete you, you give your power away. You cannot afford to make a relationship partner your savior, or you theirs. Salvation from the pit of endless need lies in one simple recognition: no one can give you what you already have.

You have been led to believe that relationships are additive: you believe you are one-half—somewhat okay, with some good points; but somewhat broken, with obvious or hidden gaps and defects. So you go searching for your other half; someone with complementary qualities and defects. You have youth and beauty, but lots of drama; he has money and stability, but is lonely. You will trade your resources, fill in each other's gaps, and together you will become whole.

Think again.

Relationships are not additive, but multiplicative. When you multiply one-half times one-half, you get one-quarter—even less than you started with. So two needy people who get together to offset each other's needs become even more needy. If you enter a relationship to offset your sense of loneliness, the relationship will only magnify your loneliness. (And there is no loneliness bleaker than being physically close with someone, yet emotionally miles away.) By contrast, whole people attract whole people and create whole relationships.

The cure for dating desperation is not to *catch* the right person, but to recognize you *are* the right person. Would you marry yourself? Do you enjoy your time with yourself enough that someone else might? If you believe you are broken, no action you take will fix you, because you started from a false premise. Before attempting to get anyone to fall in love with you, fall in love with yourself. Then you will realize you were never desperate after all. Then your dilemma will not be to find someone to love you, but to figure out what to do with all the people knocking at your door.

WHAT YOU CAN DO ABOUT IT, POINT BY POINT

- Never act out of desperation, because you are not desperate.
- Notice what you do from desperation, and ask yourself how you would act differently if you felt stronger and more confident.
- Trace weird situations or distressing results back to your choices based on desperate thinking or feeling. Next time choose from wholeness and watch your results improve.
- Give up your search for someone to complete you, for you are already whole.
- Rather than trying to catch the right person, *be* the right person.

Why You Can't Afford a Married Lover

—◆—

In a newspaper romance advice column, a forlorn reader wrote that she had fallen in love with a married man. The fellow promised to leave his wife, but kept delaying his departure. The distressed writer could not decide whether to hang in there or cut the cord.

The columnist replied with this advice: "When you are drawn to someone who is married, in the process of getting divorced, or recently divorced, imagine taking a bright-color lipstick and write on their forehead, *'Trouble.'* Such attractions usually lead to little reward and great pain."

Unhappily married people or people living with someone else or in declared committed relationships are not good candidates for a relationship. They have issues to work out. They may need to stay in their marriage or relationship, face themselves and their challenges, and find greater intimacy. Or they may need to get clear and get out. Until they do either, you are stepping into a tangled, troubled world you will probably regret getting involved in.

Attractions happen. Just think twice before you act on them. It is easy for a dissatisfied man or woman to fantasize about a better partner. He may see you as a savior from his dilemma and project onto you every wonderful attribute his partner lacks. She may swear you are soul mates and vow to love and adore you forever. This can be very tempting, especially if you are lonely or in an unsatisfying relationship yourself. Yet desperate people create desperate fantasies. Are you a real person to him, or a fantasy? And what is he to you?

Over many years I have counseled thousands of individuals and couples, privately and in seminars, and I have heard nearly every variation on dating, relationships, marriage, and divorce. I remember only a small number of situations in which someone left a marriage for someone else and it worked. Nearly every other story led to a painful outcome. There are a few exceptions, namely people in marriages that were dead (or never alive in the first place), in which the couple would have done better to split up a long time ago, or never gotten together at all. But such people represent a minority of cases.

If someone tells you they are thinking about leaving their partner or are in the process of leaving, watch to see if this is true. This process can go on for a long, long time and never come to resolution. Many married people have a hard time leaving, because they either (1) really do love their partner and want to stay; (2) really don't love their partner and can't find the courage to leave; (3) agonize over leaving, because they have a family they love; or (4) just can't make up their mind. None of these situations are healthy or attractive for you as a potential partner.

Tell such a person that you understand their position, but would prefer to participate in a clean relationship from the start. If he or she had those issues handled, you might have a chance to create a relationship, but until that happens, you don't have much to talk about. This may sound cold, especially if you feel very drawn to this person. But it's not nearly as cold as the waters you will tread if you dive in. Do not promise this person you will be there or wait for them until they clean up their marriage. They need to clean up their marriage independent of your being in the picture.

AVOID THE MISSIONARY POSITION

If you think that God has sent you to rescue this person from a pathetic predicament, awaken their passion, or teach them how to love again, get over it. While elements of your assumed purpose may be so, you are setting up your relationship for more problems than you will solve. You may indeed spark this person in a way he or she has not felt for a long time, if ever. This does not mean you are soul mates or can have a real long-term relationship. This person has deadened over the years and has hired you to play the role of the awakener. Although you hope to be the star in their movie, your role may be simply a cameo. Yes, your relationship could last. But more often it will not.

If your lover has unresolved issues in her relationship at home, the same issues will likely replicate in your relationship with her. Issues don't end by leaving. They end by changing one's mind. If your lover is shifting her attitude, value system, or lifestyle, there is hope for a new level of relationship. If she simply wants to escape the bore, bitch, or bastard, and remain the same person herself, you will be the next bore, bitch, or bastard. Are you a real person representing a real relationship, or are you an escape valve? Are you a solution, or a motivation to face the problem?

If you really want to help this person, support him to have integrity. Encourage him to speak more truth to his partner about their relationship. Do not allow him to identify you as the answer to his problems. If you are the answer to his problem now, you will be the source of his problem later. He has given his power to you, but believe me, you don't want it. His power lies within him; if he does not claim it there, he will not find it outside. When he stands strong in his true choices, everything good will flow to him. As long as he compromises his truth, wholeness will have a hard time finding him.

Your partner may also want you to be his therapist. Certainly in all good relationships partners serve as loving listeners, sounding boards, and sometimes advisers. Yet if your relationship is heavily weighted toward solving your partner's problems, you do not have a healthy platform. The best relationships are two-way streets of mutual support, and they are not founded on problem solving. If you consistently walk away feeling, "it's all about him," pay attention to this red flag.

DIVORCED BUT STILL INVOLVED

People in the process of divorce or who are recently divorced are usually not ready for an intimate or committed relationship. They are still dealing with the emotional impact of the divorce, and have lots of psychic energy cords tethered to their partner. If there are child custody and property settlement issues, there is usually a battle going on, one that you would do better not to get involved in. Such a person needs time to get clear, figure out who she is independent of the relationship, and stabilize emotionally. They usually feel angry and/or wounded and need to work through these feelings before they can be available to someone else. Starting a new relationship now may not solve their issues, but instead may complicate them. You may relieve their pain temporarily, but in the long run they need to heal from the inside out.

If you are attracted to or become friends with someone who is still emotionally involved with her ex, tread lightly and set healthy boundaries. Talk to her, enjoy her company, be her friend, and support her if you like, but do not (1) engage in activities that resemble dating; (2) become her therapist; or (3) sleep with her. Dates are for people ready to start a relationship. Therapy is for therapists. Sex is for people who can build on their time in bed. Sex for fun, relief, or release in this situation will be anything but that. It will not be fun, because there will be at least one other person in the bedroom with you emotionally (your partner's spouse). It will not be a relief to your partner, because your interlude will only muddy or delay his or her dealing with issues back home. It will not be a relief for you, because you will become emotionally involved with someone who is not available. So before pulling back the bedspread, know what you are getting into and ask yourself if you really want to go there.

IF YOU ARE THE MARRIED OR COMMITTED PERSON WHO IS HAVING AN AFFAIR

You are in a position of tremendous opportunity—not in taking a lover who will heal you, but in handling the issues within your marriage or relationship that have troubled you. You are standing at a significant crossroads in your relationship and your life. The path you take will either empower you or bring you more pain. There is a way out, if you are willing to choose it.

It is time to confront the issues that have moved you to seek a lover. Are you bored? Misunderstood? Frustrated? Lonely? Sexually unfulfilled? Are you angry and confused? Did you make a mistake in getting involved with this person? Have you grown in different directions?

If you face these questions directly and deal with them in a healthy, conscious way with your partner and/or a counselor or therapist, you will find healing and resolution beyond what a lover can offer. In maturely dealing with these situations, in most cases you can find richer love and connection with your current partner. However, in some cases you cannot, and you would be wiser to move on. In either event you will emerge with a whole heart and life, not one that is fragmented and hidden.

If you are in the process of divorce or are recently divorced, take good care of yourself. You are in or have been through an emotionally trying time, and you probably feel frayed or wounded. This is a phase for you to be with yourself, get to know who you are, and find inner peace that will establish a platform for you to make healthy new decisions. Diving into a relationship with someone quickly will most likely not serve you in the long run. It may provide momentary relief, but it will also generate more issues for you to handle, on top of the ones you are already facing. Be kind to yourself and your potential partner by treading lightly and taking the time you need to reconnect with yourself. Then, at a later time—you will know it when it comes—you can step forward with a sense of inner peace that will attract and generate the quality relationship you want and deserve.

YOU CAN HAVE IT ALL

If you have gone through a relationship with someone who is married, or are involved in such a relationship now, there are gifts you can glean from the experience. You may gain clarity on two issues: (1) you love how you feel with this person and want a relationship that feels like this; and (2) you want it with someone who is available. If you gain these insights, the relationship has served you well.

Affairs are usually more about learning than sustaining. They teach about both futility and possibility—the futility of trying to be with someone you can't have, and the possibility of finding someone you can. Why tie up your mind, heart, energy, time, and life with someone who can't give you everything you want? If you knew you could be with someone who was both attractive *and* available, wouldn't you go there quickly? Rather than bemoaning the fact that the person you are drawn to is involved or unavailable, get excited about the possibility that there is someone out there with whom you can feel these wonderful feelings who *is* available.

There *are* good people out there who are available, with whom you can share a quality relationship without lots of drama and confusion. If you are going to fantasize about a relationship, build your dream on someone who can show up. You and your lover have stimulated each other to reach for that. If you can have that with this person, you may find a way to be together in a healthy, integrated way. More likely, you will thank your partner for helping you discover what you really want, and move on to where you can have it all.

WHAT YOU CAN DO ABOUT IT, POINT BY POINT

- Think twice before getting romantically or sexually involved with someone who is married, committed, going through a divorce, or recently divorced.
- If you are attracted to such a person, ask yourself: what are the chances of this relationship going where you want to go?
- Avoid positioning yourself as your partner's savior, rescuing him or her from a bad situation.
- Encourage your partner to decide where he or she wants to go with his or her current relationship before attempting to develop a relationship with you.
- If you are married and seeking a new partner, handle the issues of your current relationship before launching out. Either stay with a whole heart or leave, but be sure you have communicated fully and come to resolution before doing so. What you seek may be available right where you are, in your current relationship.

- Know that you can have a whole relationship with someone who is available, and that you don't have to compromise to get what you want.

REASON #2.

YOU WOULD RATHER SEEK LOVE THAN FIND IT.

Many people spend a great deal of time seeking love, but few find it. Not because great love and lovers are not available, but because they do not recognize quality partners when they show up, or they keep them at arm's length. After a while the thrill, romance, or drama of seeking grows empty and you are ready to find. Are you ready to let go of seeking, so you can find?

WHAT YOU CAN DO ABOUT IT

The following chapters will show you how to:
- Identify The One you seek, and find him or her.
- Discover and move beyond limiting beliefs about relationships.
- Shift your focus from what is not working to what can work.
- Open yourself to receive more love and support in all kinds of relationships.
- Draw forth desirable traits in your dates or partner.
- Let go of fantasy relationships so that you can have a real one.

Waiting for The One

———

Seminar Participant Laura: I met a guy I like, and he asked me for a date. But I'm not sure if I should go out with him.

Alan: Why not?

Laura: I'm scared.

Alan: Scared of what?

Laura: What if we go out and we like each other? . . . Then what if we keep going out and we have sex? Then we would be really involved . . . What if we get married and have children? . . . Then what if I wake up one day and realize he's not The One?

Alan: For God's sake, it's only a date! If you don't like him, you don't have to go out with him again.

Some people get into hot water by not thinking enough about who they are dating. Others get bogged down thinking about it too much. Love, romance, relationships, and sex are matters of the heart more than the mind, about feeling more than reasoning. You can talk yourself out of happiness if you try hard enough. So give it a rest and give your love life a chance. Sometimes you just have to go with your gut and let your head catch up later.

Relationships work best when you take them step-by-step. The anxious mind wants to know where this is all headed before you set sail, but that's not always possible to know. Half the fun of a relationship is discovering it as you go along. A partner you think will be the love of your life may turn out to be a disappointing dud, while someone you would never consider ends up wowing you. You get to know potential partners—and yourself—by peeling away layers of mystery and seeing what is revealed. Often you don't know until you open the package whether it's a jewel or a booby prize. So you might as well enjoy the adventure.

GOOD AND BAD NEWS ABOUT THE ONE

Do you believe there is one perfect partner out there for you? Are you watching and waiting for your true soul mate? Do you believe in destiny?

If so, I have good news and I have bad news. The bad news is that there may not be one perfect partner out there for you. The good news is that there may be many.

For a long time I searched for The One. I left several relationships because my partner and relationship didn't measure up to my vision of The One. After I left, I discovered that I might have renounced perfection in search of it. I dated some wonderful women whom I didn't recognize as potentially magnificent partners because I was looking elsewhere.

I also know people who left relationships because they discovered The One instead. Most of those new relationships did not last very long. Fantasy is enticing, but not enduring. It's easy to project that your new partner is everything your current partner isn't. Your current or former partner has desirable traits and undesirable traits, and so does your new one. Welcome to Planet Earth. If you seek perfection, allow it to embrace your partner's humanity, complete with bald spot, stretch marks, and all. Even as you search, your perfect lover may be right beside you.

Some people recognize their soul mate the moment they meet them, and live happily ever after. That group is highly blessed and statistically insignificant. Yes, you can be among them. Just be sure that you don't miss true love while hunting for it. Don't waste a moment of joy wishing for better. Just stay open, recognize the gifts at your doorstep, and appreciate what you have before seeking other or more.

The best way to attract The One is to *be* The One. The less you value yourself, the more dangerous is your quest to find someone to fulfill you. The more you need someone to save you, the more saving you need. You do not need saving, just awakening. If you want to see The One You Have Been Waiting For, look in the mirror. Everyone else is a symbol and a substitute.

ARE YOU HEADED FOR THE ONE?

If you are not sure if your current date could be your permanent partner, here are a few tips that will help you:

1. *Lean In.* Take gentle steps at first and keep it light, easy, and freewheeling. A walk in the park, talk on the phone, or meeting at Starbucks is a healthy way to test a connection without putting yourself in a vulnerable position. Spending a short time with someone will give you clues as to whether or not you want to get to know that person better. Keep checking in with your feelings about your level of comfort and enjoyment with her. How easy is it to talk to her? Does he seem genuinely interested in getting to know you, or is he champing at the bit for sex or marriage by the end of the week? Is she upbeat and pleasant, or does she carry a lot of baggage? Is his talk tinged with sexual innuendos? Does she want to contribute to being with you, or is she a bottomless pit of need?

   After your casual meeting, there is only one question you need to answer: *Would you like to see this person again?* Put every reason for or against aside, and notice how you feel when you consider getting together again. Excited? Depressed? Attracted? Contracted? Don't think too hard about it. Connection is not about should; it's about would. Your gut will give lots of answers your head cannot fathom.

2. *Use the Truth Smoke-Out.* If you are not sure whether to spend more time with someone or get romantically, emotionally, or sexually involved, launch this request to life: *"Show me the truth about this person and relationship. If this is right and good for me, I want a sign. If not, make it clear to me."* Then relax and watch for indications; you will be amazed at what shows up. You may have an absolutely wonderful time on your next date, or you may go back to his apartment and hear messages on his answering machine from the five other women he is dating. She may be really flexible about rescheduling because you had to get your car fixed, or she may show her teeth as a raving control freak. Experience reveals character. "Ask, and you will receive" applies to life direction, and intimate relationships are no exception. A sincere request for help from higher wisdom will yield far more clarity than trying to psych out a relationship from a platform of confusion.

DO YOU FEAR MAKING A MISTAKE?

Not acting because you fear making a mistake can cost you more than making a mistake. Mistakes can often be rectified or at least not repeated. Gradually dying of loneliness is far more tragic. If you hide out in a corner and keep yourself armored before you get to know someone, you have canceled out your chances for a great connection before you even begin. Sure, there are weirdos out there to watch out for, but there are also plenty of worthwhile people whose friendship offers you gifts that far outweigh the dangers the weirdos represent.

Many people hold back from diving into relationships because their heart has been broken and they have heard war stories of others' bad experiences. While there is wisdom in discernment, there is a pitfall in overprotection. (Psychologist Alfred Adler noted, "The chief danger in life is that we take too many precautions.") Yes, watch for red flags and be prudent. But also watch for green lights and be willing. If infants feared making a mistake, they would never learn to walk—or do anything. They are willing to keep standing and falling as long as it takes to master the skill of walking. Eventually they walk for a far longer time than it took to learn. Mistakes are not the end of your world; ultimately they help you build it. The more courage you mobilize to walk beyond your fears or apprehensions, the more rapidly you will discover your right connection. If your intention is clear and strong, you will be guided.

WILL YOUR PICTURES DEVELOP?

We all have our ideas or mental pictures of how Mr. or Ms. Right will look and act. You dream of a partner with certain hair and eye colors, height, weight, profession, income, hobbies, and lifestyle. Sometimes the partner you join with will embody those traits, and sometimes he will not. I have more confidence in couples who are slightly (or greatly) mismatched than those who appear made for each other. When people seek and find someone exactly like themselves, they may just be rubber-stamping their ego and setting themselves up for psychic inbreeding. Couples who are different from each other enjoy a creative dissonance that stimulates a healthy, cutting-edge connection. Dr. Wayne Dyer recounts, "Sometimes couples tell me, *'We are like one person. We like the same food, watch the same films, read the same authors, and even dream the same dreams.'* I tell them, *'Then one of you is unnecessary.'*"

> *Life is what happens to you while*
> *you're making other plans.*
> —*John Lennon*

You may also hold a particular idea about how you will meet the love of your life, which, most likely, will not be how it happens. This may sound disappointing, but the good news is that many happy couples meet in delightfully unexpected ways. I have two friends who were set up on a blind date, basically for sex. They had each confessed to a mutual friend that they were randy and looking for a good fling. When they got together, (to their surprise) they really liked each other. Eventually they married and have had a great connection over many years (sex, too). By contrast, many people meet in traditional ways, decide that that the person before them is The One, play out their envisioned soul mate scenario, and then the relationship tanks. You can't dictate how it's supposed to unfold. Things have their own way of working out, and you do better to cooperate with what wants to happen rather than try to force love to fill a mold.

PERFECT FOR NOW

One way to soothe your fear of being with the Wrong One or missing the Perfect One is to decide if your partner can be The One for Now. Perhaps you cannot say if he is your ultimate life partner. You do not have a crystal ball, and you have your doubts if you can or will go the distance with this person. But you *can* say if you want to be with him today—and sometimes that is all you need to know. Relationships, like life, are built one day at a time; if the relationship is good today, it is good.

While many of us quest for a lifetime mate, sometimes we have different mates at different stages of our life. Temporary mates can be just as important as lifetime partners. In a way, lifetime partners are also temporary, since one day you will part physically. So the duration of your time together does not matter as much as the quality of that time. Sometimes short-term connections are more profound and life enhancing than long-term ones. That is why it is important to make every relationship count, no matter whether it lasts for a weekend or a lifetime.

If you are in a relationship with dangling question marks about your purpose or longevity, you might say to your partner, "*I am not sure if you are my ultimate life partner, but I do very much enjoy being with you. If you are willing to be with me on that basis, our time can be really worthwhile.*"

Relationships in this scenario may evolve in a number of directions:

1. Some live out their purpose and both partners move on to other relationships. Often such couples remain

friends because their relationship was founded in honesty and respect, and partners appreciate the contribution they made to each other's lives.

2. One partner gets hurt because they were hoping for more, and when more did not pan out, they feel disappointed or devastated. This is why it is so important to be completely honest about where you stand and what you want. If you are not sure if you want to be with someone for the distance, say so. If you do know, say so. Harboring the hidden agenda that someday you will be together even though you are not quite together now can undermine your joy now and later. Celebrating the riches you do own together will bring you fulfillment now and lead to greater fulfillment later, even if you end up with a different partner.

3. The relationship catches fire. One day you look at your partner, your heart flies open, and you realize that you deeply love her.

4. You gradually fall in love with each other. Over time, you share life's joys and sorrows, open more of your real selves to each other, weather difficulties, and your roots grow together. You form a bond that runs deeper and surer than first-blush titillation, and you "drink from the cup that lovers own."

5. One day it hits you that your life is far better with
   your partner than without her. Despite your reservations and resistance, you realize you have a good
   thing going, and your exit strategies evaporate in the
   face of the incontrovertible truth that this is
   working.

Any of these scenarios is preferable to ditching or squashing
the relationship because you're not sure if you will end up
together. If you are willing to let him be The One for Now, this
pleasing moment leads to many more pleasing moments, and
you may stay together for a long time by surfing on the cutting
edge of such pleasing moments. Each day you decide that he is
a good one for today, and you stay together by ongoing conscious choice—not just because you said you would.

DON'T STAND SHIVERING IN FRONT OF THE FIRE

While obsessively seeking Mr. or Ms. Right appears to be an
avenue to creating a relationship, it may be a way of *avoiding*
relationship. Your fantasy may breed excuses for not appreciating your life as it is, and your dream lover may be a distraction from love rather than its fulfillment. Your hunt for a mate
may be exactly what keeps your mate at a distance, and you
stand shivering in the cold while a warm hearth is but feet
away. Although many people truly want love, fewer are willing
to receive it.

Earlier I noted that true love is less about *finding* the right
person and more about *being* the right person. Here we might
add that true love is less about finding the right person and

more about *letting someone be* the right person. With but a shift in perception, what you thought was miles or lifetimes away may be but feet and moments away—or right in your arms.

To transform your dream lover from a fantasy to a reality, practice finding love where you stand. Celebrate the gifts in the people you date, your friends, family, business associates, and, most important, yourself. Quit waiting for the future joy and blessings The One will bring, and find the present joy and blessings that have already been delivered to you. I promise you they are many. Then, when you are immersed in the abundance at hand, someone will tap you on the shoulder at the most unexpected moment, and you will find that all the simple moments of loving have led to a more momentous one.

WHAT YOU CAN DO ABOUT IT, POINT BY POINT

- Give dates and relationships a chance to reveal what they can offer you. Beware of red flags, but don't overlook green ones.
- To gauge where a relationship might be headed, lean in, keep it light at first, watch for signs, and respect your gut feelings.
- Sometimes your pictures turn out as you expect, and often they don't. Let life surprise and delight you.
- The fastest road to Mr. or Ms. Right may be to enjoy Mr. or Ms. Right Now.
- If you fear making a mistake, just take your relationship day by day, choosing as you go.
- Appreciate who and what is before you before asking for more.

"All the Good Ones Are Taken or Gay"

———∾———

Coaching Client Kristin: I'm afraid I'll never find a decent guy. All the good ones are taken or gay.

Alan: Now there's an affirmation that will keep you stuck.

Kristin: It seems that everyone I meet is either in a relationship or not emotionally available.

Alan: How many men do you want, anyway?

Kristin: One would do.

Alan: Can you believe there is at least one available man out there whom you want, and who wants you?

Kristin: Well, that sounds possible.

Alan: Opening up even a little crack in your belief system can make space for a great partner.

While driving to work daily with my friend Stephen, we would talk about women and relationships. Stephen was happily married and I was trying to be happily single, and we had plenty of time sitting in Los Angeles freeway (ha!) traffic to debate the relative merits of husbandry versus bachelorhood. I told Stephen that my experience dating women was that they started out as cuddly as Strawberry Shortcake, but sooner or later morphed into the Wicked Witch of the West. "Have you found that, too?" I asked Stephen, expecting he would agree. To my surprise, he answered, "No, I have not found that to be true. I had good experiences with women before my marriage, and my wife is very supportive of me."

My knee-jerk reaction was to want to argue my case—and I had plenty of wounded-in-action stories to back it up. But instead I tried to see the situation from his perspective: Here was a guy whose experience of women was entirely different from mine. Plus, he had a good marriage over many years. If an absolute truth about women existed, we couldn't *both* be right. So I decided I would rather have him be right. At least then I stood a chance for a happy relationship. The more I thought about it, the more I recognized that I had been living under a belief that didn't serve me—and I didn't want that belief anymore.

From that time on, my pattern changed. My relationships with women yielded more joy and less warfare, and didn't turn sour. When I changed my mind, so did my relationships. That conversation with Stephen was a turning point for me. His big picture annihilated my little one, and suddenly I was living in a larger world.

LACK OR SUPPLY?

One of the most self-defeating dating beliefs is a belief in the lack or short supply of available men or women to date. Many times I have heard women commiserate, "All the good ones are taken or gay." While this may often be said in half-jest, it is often said in half-truth. When your well-meaning, supportive friends agree with you, that half-truth expands to whole truth, and your world tragically shrinks.

> *A conclusion is a place where*
> *you got tired of thinking.*
> —*Stephen Wright*

You do not realize how powerful your mind is. *It is literally generating your world.* If you think "victim" or "poor me" thoughts, you live as if you are poor, even if you are not. In coaching sessions I often encounter clients who respond to a suggestion with a hasty, "Yes, but . . ." and then fill in a reason why the idea isn't sound. I approach from another angle, and again they reply, "Yes, but . . .". I then try one more time with a different tack. If I get another "Yes, but . . . ," I realize they have more of an investment in their issue than in the solution. Then I kick them in their "Yes, but . . .". I tell them I cannot help them unless they are willing to receive help. They need to reduce the size of their "But . . .".

In a seminar a woman named Jan recounted a long, woeful tale about how her twenty-one-year-old daughter, still living at home, was highly irresponsible and abusing her household. Yet Jan felt too guilty about setting even a few reasonable boundaries that would make her home life easier. It was clear to me that Jan needed to tell her daughter she would either have to respect her mother's household rules or get her own place. Yet in the face of my various suggestions, Jan had a long list of reasons why this situation couldn't be resolved. Finally I told her, "I can help you, but if you are not open to help, I cannot. Are you willing to work with me? If not, I will move on."

Suddenly Jan "got it" and agreed to do an exercise with me. We role-played a scene in which Jan had a highly productive conversation with her daughter. During the exercise Jan became so authoritative that the audience gave her a huge ovation. She had tapped into her power to lovingly yet firmly say "no" to abusive behavior. When she became willing, she shifted.

When you are open to receive a better relationship than you have experienced, the universe will deliver it. Like Jan, you will have to get off your "But . . .". The more you focus on who is not there, the more no one is there. The more you focus on who is there or who might be there, the more you increase your chances of someone great showing up in your life.

The partners available to you are less a result of what's going on out there and more a result of what's going on in your head and heart. You have probably heard that your most crucial sex organ is your brain; it is the same for romance and relationships. Because your beliefs both limit and liberate your experience, your date or mate can find their way to you only if you let them in.

Think you can or think you can't,
and either way you will be correct.
—*Henry Ford*

You may have tried many methods to create a rewarding relationship, but you may have never examined the assumptions that build a wall between you and that relationship. Many people would rather be right about what's wrong than test their beliefs. They will defend to the death why things are not working, without considering how things could work if they let them. They believe that the outside world is doing it to them or for them rather than taking responsibility for the crucial link between beliefs and results. When you hook up those two factors, you are well on your way to freedom. Below are some of the most important beliefs to call to question:

Top 20 Excuses for Not Having a Great Relationship
- (Men) (Women) suck.
- I've had too many bad experiences—or one really bad one—to trust someone again.
- I need to resolve my core issues instilled by the negative programming I received as a child.
- I am paying off karma for being mean to (women) (men) in a previous life.

- When Venus aligns with Mars in the third house . . .
- I am too old, fat, or unattractive.
- No one would want me with kids.
- I can't afford one.
- The people at the social gatherings I attend are losers.
- I'm still paying alimony for the last one.
- I can't get the last one to pay alimony.
- If someone knew the truth about me, they would not want me.
- I like my privacy/space too much.
- I'm too busy.
- The (guys) (women) I date are not spiritual enough.
- My kids don't like anyone I date.
- I don't want to play the role of my partner's mother.
- Guys just want sex.
- Women nag.
- Whatever God wills . . .

BOGUS BELIEF BUSTERS

Okay, you have identified one or several of your limiting beliefs in the list above. Or you are aware of others not mentioned. Now what? How do you break free to create a more expansive awareness, and let someone in?

1. *Tell the truth about how you feel about relationships.* Are you still pissed off at the dork who ditched you? Do you equate intimacy with the Texas chainsaw massacre? Have you gotten so used to doing things your way that if someone hung the toilet paper in the

wrong direction, it would upset your world? Are you having too much fun screwing around to give it up? Do you like the romance of starting relationships, but hate the issues it leads to?

Take a few moments to fill in the blanks below and after each of the following points to get in touch with where you stand and what you want. There are no right or wrong answers. Simple honesty will be your best friend here. (Feel free to record your responses on a separate piece of paper or your computer if you prefer.)

*What I believe about relationships:*_____.
*How I feel about relationships:*_____.

The best possible time to be alive is when almost everything you thought you knew is wrong!
—*Tom Stoppard*

---

2. *Hold your belief up to question.* Are you so sure all the good ones are taken or gay? Have you ever met a good one who is not taken or gay? Would you be willing to be wrong about what is not working so you can have what you want?

*I am willing to question and challenge my belief that*_____.

3. *Pay attention to people who have what you want.* Do you know anyone who has found someone both attractive and available? How did they do it? Are they an exception to a condition of lack, or is the same supply available to you? Focus on cases that prove that your goal is possible to achieve. If you can see it for someone else, you can see and have it yourself.

*People or couples I know who demonstrate I can have what I want:*_____

_____.

4. *When you find yourself in a conversation asserting lack, make a statement affirming supply or remain silent.*

Female friend: *I'm never going on Match.com again. All the guys are liars or perverts.*

You (female): *I once met a nice guy there who was pretty honest. We had some good conversations and ended up dating for quite awhile.*

Male friend: *I just broke up with Susie. All she did was bitch. Women are so high-maintenance.*

You (male): *I know how you feel. I used to think that, too, until I started dating Sandy. She's really easy to be with.*

Group (female): *We're so over guys. They just use you and then dump you for someone better.*

You: [Remain silent, change the subject, or step out of the room.]

*A statement of supply I want to affirm:*_____.

5. *Choose friends who affirm abundance.* If your friends continually complain about lack and argue for their limits, you may want to find some new friends whose conversations point toward possibilities. Hanging out with friends is like eating a meal. If it is tasty and nutritious, you walk away happy and full. If the ingredients are inferior or poisoned, you feel crummy or sick afterward. The company you keep represents where you are headed, so choose your company wisely.

    *Friends who support me to have all I want:*_____.

6. *Nurture yourself.* Get regular massages, order Chardonnay in between birthdays, rent that beach house in Aruba, and play with people who make you laugh. Visit your family only if you want to. Dump any ideas your parents or religion told you about how much you have to suffer before you can have what you want; if that were true, they would be happy themselves. Self-nurturing will amplify your sense of opulence and open you to an abundant supply of potential partners.

> *Give yourself abundant pleasure,*
> *that you may have abundant*
> *pleasure to give others.*
> —*Neale Donald Walsch*

*What I can do to love and nurture myself:*_____.

Your world is as large or as small as you let it be. You can build a whole world on limiting assumptions and keep finding proofs for it. You can also build a world on open-ended possibilities and it will prove itself. There are lots of people out there you can have if you want them. Not all the good ones are taken or gay. One of them may be seeking you at this very moment.

WHAT YOU CAN DO ABOUT IT, POINT BY POINT

- Examine and question your beliefs of "not enough" when it comes to dates and relationships.
- Quit arguing for the limited way things are, and make a stand for the way they could be.
- Observe people who have what you want, and honor them as role models.
- Choose friends who agree with your possibilities rather than your limits.
- Create self-nurturing activities that affirm you can have what you want and deserve.

Looking for Wrong
in All the Love Places

———~~~———

Seminar Participant Wendy: I deeply want to connect with my soul mate, but I haven't been able to.

Alan: Tell me about your relationships.

Wendy: Men are immature and basically incapable of relationships. They have no idea how to treat a woman. Most of them just want sex. One guy I went out with rambled on about his ex-wife. Another wanted me to pay for myself. Another was never on time. Do you see what I have to put up with?

Alan: I'm not surprised you haven't attracted someone. Your words say that you want a man, but your energy is tied up in reasons why you can't have one.

Wendy: I have good luck helping other people get together.

Alan: What line of work are you in?

Wendy: I run a dating service.

Wendy sincerely wanted a mate. But her judgments and negative expectations about men were so heavily weighted against them that no man could pass through the minefield of her beliefs. Given such a prejudice, Wendy would either keep attracting men with undesirable traits, or find things wrong with men who might have a lot to offer her. Wendy drew her conclusions from the evidence she gathered, but the part of her mind that gathered the evidence was tainted by her history and projections. Thus she set up a no-win situation, rendering her "right"—but unhappy.

In the last chapter, we looked at limiting beliefs based on lack, or feeling "The odds are against me." Now we will expose and move beyond a related belief: "The odds are good, but the goods are odd." There may be lots of potential partners out there, but if there is something wrong with all of them—or you think there is—you cut off your chances before you begin, and you find yourself in that all-too-familiar dismal position—alone again, naturally.

PICKY, PICKY, PICKY

A friend of the Sufi "rascal sage" Nasrudin asked him why he had never gotten married.

"All of the significant women in my life have had tragic flaws," explained Nasrudin.

"Like what?"

"First there was Samantha from London. She was very sweet, but her nose was quite large. I couldn't get beyond it. Olga the Russian heiress was gorgeous, but a dull lover. Then there was Stella, an Italian. She was passionate, but emotionally volatile."

"Have you ever met a woman you thought you could be with?" asked Nasrudin's friend.

"Ah, yes," Nasrudin replied with a sigh. "Ingrid from Sweden was perfect in every way. She was stunningly attractive, good-natured, and an awesome lover—my dream woman, down to every detail."

"Then why didn't you marry her?" asked the friend.

"She was looking for a perfect man," Nasrudin explained.

After I broke up with a girlfriend (following other breakups), my buddy Barry showed me a cartoon of a skeleton sitting on a park bench. The caption read, "Waiting for Ms. Right." Gulp. Was I canceling out great opportunities because I was being too picky, finding things wrong where there was a lot more that was right?

> *Those who go searching for love only find their own lovelessness. But the loveless never find love; only the loving find love, and they never have to search for it.*
>
> —D. H. Lawrence

Much as I hated to admit it, I was missing out on the best part of relationships, because I was paying more attention to blemishes than beauty. Though I earnestly sought love, I feared it more. One way to keep intimacy at a distance is to target flaws in a partner before he or she gets too close. Though many of us would not like to admit it, relationships mirror our intentions. If you have had a string of painful or disappointing relationships and you complain that you have not found what you are looking for, consider that you *have* found what you are looking for—you have been looking for what is wrong, and found plenty of it.

A Course in Miracles, published by the Foundation for Inner Peace, tells us that the ego's motto is "seek and do not find." The motto of the heart, or spirit, is "seek and find," or simply, "find." People who constantly seek and never find are more committed to seeking than finding. Regardless of the circumstances upon which you blame your sense of limits or injustice, your results stem not from external conditions, but from internal choices.

ARE YOU LETTING LIFE LOVE YOU?

One question can change your life in a huge way if you answer it honestly:

Are you letting life love you?

Do you allow good things into your life, or do you push them away when they show up, finding more faults than gifts? Do you bury your pain and loneliness, and work until you are too tired to play? Do you complain about what is wrong with potential partners to the point that you set up an invisible force field that repels someone desirable when they approach?

Could you have the relationship you dream of, if you let someone in?

When you are ready and willing, one sincere "yes" can undo a long string of "no's." When your desire exceeds your resistance, it will happen easily, naturally, and without struggle. Here are some ways you can open yourself to a great love relationship by practicing to let life love you:

- Receive compliments gratefully and graciously.
- Let other people treat you to dinner when they offer.
- Accept help when others offer.
- Schedule regular massages, fun trips, and mini-vacations.
- Buy the hot tub you have been thinking about.
- Say yes to a date with someone you like, or ask that person out.
- Let someone else do the dishes for a change.
- Take breaks during your day; put your feet up; lie in the sun; listen to your favorite music.
- Don't look at the prices when ordering from a menu.
- Enjoy sex without psyching it out and analyzing what it means.
- Take yourself to dinner or a movie even if you don't have a friend to go with.
- Let someone wonderful into your heart and life.

PERFECTLY IMPERFECT

When Josh heard Jennifer sing at a concert, he fell in love with her on the spot. The two dated and married and have enjoyed a deeply devoted relationship for many years. Yet even they have their issues. Jennifer once told me, "Sometimes I feel annoyed with Josh's idiosyncrasies. I even thought about leaving him. But then I realized that I have no right to demand perfection, because I cannot offer it." Behold two human beings, with all their magnificence and all their faults—like all of us. Even while quirks and character defects exist, how much can you find to love and appreciate?

If you scout for imperfections, you will find them. If you scout for perfections, you will find them. A friend of mine noted, "I used to think I was a perfectionist, because I noticed little flaws in everyone and everything. Then I realized I was really an *imperfectionist*. If I was a perfectionist, I would notice what was perfect."

At every moment you are making up who your partner is, who you are, and what your relationship is. If you are happy in your relationship, you are giving that gift to yourself. If you are finding fault, you are giving that to yourself. Your partner is simply acting out the movie you are producing. You have the power to rewrite the script if you choose.

HOW TO CALL FORTH THE PARTNER YOU WANT

A college psychology class schemed to practice their lessons on their professor, who had a habit of pacing back and forth in front of the class while he lectured. The students decided to reward Dr. Kensington for staying on the left side of the classroom, but not the right. When the teacher stood on the left, the students sat up, paid attention, took notes, asked questions, and laughed at his jokes. When the professor paced to the right, they withdrew their attention, gazed aimlessly around the room, asked no questions, and looked bored. It was not long before Dr. Kensington was spending all of his time teaching from the left.

Give them a reputation to live up to!
—Dale Carnegie

Likewise, you can influence your partner to bring forth his or her most desirable traits. Here are some tips:

- Relate to him as if he is the person you want him to be rather than the person you fear or resist.
- When she behaves in a way you appreciate, compliment her immediately and refer to it again later.
- Do not harp on the behaviors you do not like.
- Do not reinforce your image of him as a problem by complaining to others and rehashing stories.
- Each day take a minute or two by yourself (preferably at the start of the day) and visualize the best in your partner. Think of all the things you appreciate, and watch a mental movie of how great your relationship is, or could be.

Your attention is the strongest currency at your disposal. Whatever you invest it in will reap greater returns of like kind. If you implement the simple tips above, you will be amazed at how the best in your partner comes forth.

Successful relationships are not a mystery. They operate on universal principles that you can make work on your behalf. On your next date or in your next relationship, practice finding what you want. This may sound simplistic, but it may be the one key you have overlooked. Even if you have one date with someone and you decide not to see her again, don't waste your evening by complaining to yourself about who she is not, or what she can't offer you. Instead, be thankful for the bright moments and any fun you have. If you cultivate this attitude, you will quickly draw to you more and more people who will offer you what you want. Then you will recognize that it is not *they* who are giving you gifts, but *you* who are giving them to yourself.

When your intention to enjoy your mate is strong, you will attract someone with a strong intention to enjoy you as his or her mate. The signal you send determines the signal you will receive. Rather than manipulating people or events, refine your signal. People and events will line up in synchronistic, even miraculous ways when your investment to get what you want outshines your focus on what is missing.

WHAT YOU CAN DO ABOUT IT, POINT BY POINT

- Pay more attention to what is working than what is broken, and edify your focus with like words and thoughts.
- Practice letting life love you by graciously accepting compliments, gifts, and love, and by engaging in self-nurturing activities.
- Accept your dates or partner as human beings, with both great qualities and imperfections.
- Draw forth the best in your partner by rewarding him or her for behaviors you value and withdrawing your attention from behaviors you do not like.
- Be a love finder rather than a love seeker.

The Attraction
of Fantasy Lovers

—◆—

I once presented a weekend seminar at a retreat center staffed by Catholic nuns. Several weeks later I received a phone call from one of the seminar participants. Gary was going through a personal crisis and wanted some counseling. When I met with him, he explained his predicament:

Gary: I am in love and I don't know what to do.

Alan: Who are you in love with?

Gary: Sister Barbara.

Alan: Sister Barbara? The nun?

Gary: Yes, Sister Barbara. We are very much in love.

Alan: She told you she was in love with you?

Gary: She didn't really say it outright. But I can tell. We had chemistry.

Alan: So what did you do?

Gary: I phoned her a few times, but she denied her feelings. She must be going through terrible turmoil trying to reconcile her profession of faith with her attraction to me.

Alan: How do you know all this?

Gary: I can feel it.

Alan: What did she tell you?

Gary: She got mad and told me never to call her again.

Alan: Gary, are you sure Sister Barbara is in love with you?

Gary: Of course she is. Otherwise why would she get so upset when I kept calling her?

I would bet big money that Gary's love affair with Sister Barbara did not lead to a flaming romance. Their "soul mate connection" was his wishful fantasy. Gary was no wide-eyed bohemian teenager, mind you—he was a mature, respectable computer executive. He just really wanted to be in love, and a nun seemed safer to him than a vivacious woman he would have to deal with up close and personal. Rather than choosing someone who was geographically or emotionally unavailable, he chose someone who was religiously unavailable. *Whatever works* . . .

We have all had crushes at a distance and made up stories about people we wished would love us. Fantasizing about the perfect lover generates a terrific romantic rush—without having to face the challenges of relating to a real human being on a daily basis. A crush is exhilarating; juicy endorphins flood your system and you feel elated. How wonderful to be in love! Your beloved person may not even know of your love—or that you even exist—but that doesn't matter. You feel tickled from inside out, and your life has a greater purpose than making it home in time for reruns of *Friends*.

Eventually, however, reality rears its earthy head and you begin to feel the frustration of not being with the object of your heart's desire. At that point you may choose one of several paths:

1. You make your move to get with this person, and he either blows you off or opens to connect with you.
2. You realize there is no way this person will be your lover, and you quit your pursuit. You let go, get a life, and choose a relationship with someone you can touch.
3. You redouble your efforts and pursue your "soul mate" more fervently, even to the point of stalking her.
4. You find faults with your dream lover so that you can justify pushing him away. You may confront and criticize him and/or badmouth him to others.

5. You give up pursuing your dream soul mate, but live in a fantasy of one day being with her, at the expense of developing a real-life relationship.

A LOVER YOU CAN WRAP YOUR ARMS AROUND

My partner, Dee, has been a Barry Manilow fan for many years. When she learned of an upcoming Manilow concert in Las Vegas, we decided to go. Little did I know I was in for one of the best self-help seminars of my life. The moment The Golden Boy vaulted onstage in his maroon velvet tails, a colossal shriek issued from the crowd . . . ten thousand wild and crazy women pining for a shot at a nice Jewish boy.

My moment of insight came when two diehard fans sat down next to me. The woman closest to me sat for the entire concert with a dazed, glazed look in her eyes, her jaw agape. There was no question that Barry Manilow was her fantasy lover of a lifetime, her True Soul Mate appointed by God. She would never touch Barry, have a conversation with him, or be in his hundred-dollar-a-seat presence again for a long time. But he was clearly The One, and he was singing soulful love songs just to her. The woman's expression reminded me of stories I have read about people in prisoner-of-war camps who survive by imagining themselves on a tropical island. But we were not in a prison camp; we were in Las Vegas.

Imagination is a healthy way to cope with stress when there is no other escape. But when it becomes a substitute for living, it morphs to tragedy. In *Barry Manilow: The Biography* (Music

Sales Corp., 2002), writer Patricia Butler records some of Barry's ardent fans' soul mate fantasies. Take Rosie, a forty-three-year-old British housewife:

> *Me and my husband only live together now as brother and sister. . . . I just feel unclean with any other man apart from Barry. If I can't have sexual intercourse with Barry, I'll go without. I'll never be unfaithful to Barry. . . . Barry kisses me goodnight . . . and I think, "Oh, if only I could wave a magic wand and make these posters come to life." . . . [My friend] Patricia's husband said: "I think it's quite ridiculous you being so addicted to a man you're never going to meet. . . . You've got to choose between me and Barry. . . . so they split up . . . If Barry had lived 2,000 years ago who would you say he was? . . . I think he's the second coming. . . . People who aren't fans of Barry . . . think: "Well, he's laughing all the way to the bank, getting richer and richer; you're getting poorer and poorer." . . . I say, "No, Barry is getting richer financially, we're getting richer morally."*

Although this example is extreme, it illustrates a dynamic that many of us have experienced to some degree, on either the giving or the receiving end. Giving your heart, body, mind, and spirit to someone you will never meet is not a sign of moral riches, but of emotional poverty. You are saying, in effect, "My life and relationships suck so badly that I cannot imagine having the kind of love I deeply desire. So I am throwing in the towel on my real life and taking refuge in a fantasy lover."

I have given up my search for truth,
and would settle for a good fantasy.
                                    —*Ashleigh Brilliant*

Barry Manilow, like other inspired entertainers, elicits romance and passion from his fans—a rare and precious gift to those who seek more love in their lives. The question is, how can fans sustain that passion on a regular basis, rather than waiting until the once a year when Santa Barry slides down the chimney? Will kissing a poster get them what they really want, or would they do better to kiss a real person they can wrap their arms around? Can they find electricity in and around a more available person, rather than waiting for Barry to deliver their fix?

Let's return for a moment to the prison camp analogy: If your only resort to your current boring or conflicted relationship is an active fantasy world, you must feel terribly imprisoned, with no reward or way out. So you silently put up with hell and relegate heaven to your private imaginings. In a way the formula is wise, for you have found an avenue to give yourself pleasure in a world of pain, and your method may enable you to survive for now. Yet there is one crucial possibility you have overlooked: *Change your life so that you bring real love into it* rather than seeking for it over the blue horizon. Take the passion and aspiration you pointed toward an intangible savior, and redirect it toward a relationship that can fulfill you right where you stand. Such a quest may feel shaky, frightening, or threatening, yet the payoff is huge. You will be trading an imaginary love life for a real one.

SOUL MATE SIGNS

In your quest for Mr. or Ms. Right, you may receive fortuitous signals that your crush is justified, some of them so serendipitous that you are certain God has delivered them.

When I was searching for my soul mate, I opened a magazine containing an article about an artist, including her photo. I was immediately drawn to this woman, and could not take my eyes off her picture, which emanated both physical beauty and soul qualities I yearned for. I fell in love with her on the spot, knowing nothing about her but her image and the brief information in the article. Immediately I decided she was my soul mate and I would marry her.

The next day I was driving with my buddy Charley, who noticed the magazine in my car and began to peruse it. When he reached the page with the artist's photo, he stared at it for a minute, pointed to the picture, and remarked seriously, "There's your woman, Alan." My heart leaped! I had said nothing to Charley about the woman, and there were no dog-ears or markings on the page (or other telltale spots). Here was a confirmation if ever there was one!

I contacted the artist and made an appointment to meet her. She was happy to hear from me and told me she had once attended one of my lectures. *A sign.* When we got together and she showed me around her studio, she pointed out a painting with the title of one of my books. *Another sign.* We spent a lovely afternoon together and had a lot to talk about. I was in heaven. *How many signs do you need?* The universe had clearly guided me to this woman, and my dream was coming true before my eyes.

When we met again the next day, I told her that I felt attracted to her and wanted to explore a relationship. She told me that she, too, enjoyed our time together, and, were she not in a committed relationship, there might be some possibilities for us. *Crash.* I inquired more about her relationship, and she indeed seemed fulfilled.

Later that year I wrote to her to find out if she was still with her partner, and she informed me that she and her beloved were building their dream home. *Beginning of her dream, end of mine.*

In retrospect, that experience was a milestone lesson for me. I learned how easily my mind could make up a story and generate amazing confirmations. In the case of Charley's corroboration over her photograph, I believe he was not reading some universal destiny, but my thoughts and feelings. My psychic energy was so invested in that photo that he picked up on it and unknowingly reflected it back to me. (Children, animals, and highly sensitive people do this all the time.)

I have also had numerous women come to me with mind-boggling substantiations that I was their life partner: dreams in which Jesus appointed us to be together; psychic predictions that she would marry an author from Hawaii; special songs playing on the radio as she was thinking of me; and on and on. Although I respected these women for following their hearts and speaking their truth, all I could answer was that I did not receive the same guidance and did not sense we were to be life partners. And we weren't.

How, then, can you know if your signs and intuitions are correct? Easy: *if you get together and it works, your signs were right.* If, on the other hand, the other person is not interested or available, stop there. If you keep pushing after that point, you have seen *Notting Hill* one too many times.

Here are some signs that your idealized lover is worth pursuing:

- He is a real person in your circle of friends or associates, with whom you do or can have meaningful contact.
- You can have a genuine conversation with her, beyond "Hi, how ya doin'?" or a brief interchange at the water cooler.
- He is not married or in a relationship.
- She is mentally, emotionally, geographically, and religiously available.
- He expresses an interest in you.
- You feel open and ready to be with her.

Here are some signs that your lover is more of a fantasy than a reality:

- He is a celebrity or dwells in a circle far distant from your own.
- She is virtually impossible to get in touch with or to have a two-way communication with.
- He is married, in a relationship, a hopeless workaholic, lives in Mongolia, has taken a vow of celibacy, or is a "bad boy" with misogynistic tendencies.
- She is in considerable pain over a current or past breakup.
- He has not expressed a particular interest in you, and/or you exaggerate a tiny shred of possible interest so that it seems dominant.

- You would freak out if she actually showed up and wanted you.

GHOSTS MAKE LOUSY LOVERS

Romantic movies do relationships a great injustice by inferring that you have to overcome impossible odds to capture your dream lover. Yet you do not need to scale the Himalayas to find your true love; your chances are far better if he or she lives within driving distance.

Reality is that which, when you stop
believing in it, doesn't go away.
—*Philip K. Dick*

What good is being in love if you can't wrap your arms around your lover? If someone is physically or emotionally unavailable, you can't really claim you have a relationship. You have an idea for a relationship, but an idea cannot breathe sexy whispers in your ear; trail hot, moist kisses down your neck; and toss you around in bed until all the sheets are rumpled on the floor. Sure, you can masturbate physically or emotionally to a fantasy (and your orgasm may surpass some you have had with real people). But that is no excuse to relegate your beloved to a remote island in your mind with no commuter service from where you stand.

What you are asking for is not outrageous; what you are settling for is. As long as you are absorbed in a fantasy lover, you deny yourself a real one. Thank your dream partner for opening your heart or keeping it alive, but then apply passion liberally right where you stand. Your soul is too precious to invest in a myth; reinvest it in someone who can give you a return. If you let a living, breathing person into your heart, your fantasy lover will come to life in your own arms and bed, and you won't have to fall for a woman already married to God or pay a hundred dollars to see your fantasy man once a year from the eighty-third row.

WHAT YOU CAN DO ABOUT IT, POINT BY POINT

- Decide where you stand on the above list of character-istics of real versus fantasy lovers.
- Recognize that a crush on a fantasy lover does not yield the joy and fulfillment a relationship with a real person at your side.
- Consider through introspection or counseling why having a real-life lover or relationship may be fright-ening or threatening to you.
- If you have been holding a crush, do a release cere-mony in which you tear up the person's picture and/or symbolically or ritually release and say good-bye to him or her.
- Refocus your attention and energy toward someone available with whom you can build a rewarding day-to-day relationship.

REASON #3.

YOU LET PAST PAIN KEEP YOU FROM PRESENT LOVE.

Nearly everyone has suffered a broken heart at one time or another. Some people move on to create new and better relationships, while others are so steeped in pain, resentment, anger, or guilt that they repel happy relationships from finding their way to them. This need not be. No matter how badly you have been wounded, you can move beyond the pain to enjoy a far more rewarding relationship.

WHAT YOU CAN DO ABOUT IT

The following chapters will show you how to:

- Recognize if and how you may be letting a past relationship stand between you and great love.
- Release a painful past partner or relationship and move on.
- Deal with relationships that seem too good to be true.
- Decide whether or not to get back with a former partner, and how to do it.
- Break a cycle of repetitious unsuccessful relationship patterns and upgrade to a new and more rewarding level.
- Appreciate all of your relationships as stepping-stones to get you where you want to go.

Healing a Wounded Heart

~~~

When Elizabeth's husband, Tim, cheated on her, she was devastated. Divorce proceedings followed quickly, then a long, messy battle over alimony, child support, and custody of their son.

After the divorce Elizabeth became a hermit. Wounded badly, she hardly went out even with her friends, let alone men. Elizabeth watched lots of TV, put on a few pounds, and practically became addicted to doing Sudoku puzzles. She grew cynical about men and distanced herself from guys she worked with. If any of them brought up the subject of relationships, even innocently, she fired back a sarcastic comment.

Eventually Elizabeth felt lonely and decided to date again. Yet her dates were fiascos; some of the guys were nice but blah, and the others, well . . . they were typical self-involved males.

When Elizabeth came to me for help, she realized that she could not see men clearly, because she superimposed her ex-husband's face over everyone she dated. Not that she wanted to get back with Tim; their marriage was history. But before she could build a healthy relationship with a new partner, she had to get beyond the anger and resentment she felt toward Tim and overcome the victim position she had adopted. Elizabeth was bearing a "treasured wound."

Elizabeth courageously got together with Tim and told him she was ready to let go of her animosity, and that she sincerely wanted a more harmonious relationship. During the time since their marriage, Tim had grown and changed, too. He apologized for his mistakes and wished Elizabeth well.

Elizabeth came to our next coaching session glowing. She looked lighter and freer than I had ever seen her. Soon after that Elizabeth began to date, and she developed a relationship with a man she found attractive. The last time I heard from Elizabeth, she was engaged. When she decided to let go, she opened the door to a new and better relationship.

One of Charles Dickens's most memorable characters is the eccentric spinster Miss Havisham. We meet Miss Havisham in *Great Expectations* as she dons a tattered, ancient wedding gown and sits down to dine on rotting china at a creaky banquet table showcasing a cobwebbed cake. These pathetic symbols serve as her macabre reminders of the day she was jilted at the altar thirty years earlier. Miss Havisham is perhaps the saddest icon of treasured wounds, as she daily reinstates her historical agony at the expense of present or future love.

Yet Miss Havisham's caricature is not terribly exaggerated from the way many of us cling to past hurts as badges of relationship sorrow. "See how horribly she devastated me!" we announce with bent demeanor. Or, "If it were not for him, I would be happy now." Yet it is not her or him that makes us unhappy now. It is the baggage we cling to that tethers us to the past, a chain forged with links of resentment and fear.

After my book *Happily Even After* was published, I received an angry letter from a fellow who was involved in a support group for victims of extramarital affairs. He lambasted a chapter in the book titled "An Affair to Remember," in which I proposed that you can grow beyond the heartache of infidelity by reframing it. Rather than regarding an affair as a disaster, I suggested, you can use it to learn and grow. When a partner strays, he or she is making a statement about the lack of fulfillment he or she felt in the relationship, an unaddressed fear or resistance, or a weakness in that bond. When an affair comes to light, it can motivate a couple to revisit their relationship, recognize and acknowledge their unspoken feelings, communicate more honestly, and either part by choice or deepen the relationship so that it becomes stronger than it was before the incident.

Well, this reader and his group were not exactly pleased as punch with that suggestion. In fact, they were damn pissed off that I would even suggest that some good could come from such a horrible experience. Yes, betrayal sucks. Most of us have felt burned by someone and bear the scars to prove it. But what's the use in continuing to relive the ordeal and beat its angry drum to the point that you can't hear any new music? At some point, after you have felt, addressed, and learned from the pain, it is time to move on. Otherwise you just hurt yourself.

> *It is not the love we did not receive in*
> *the past that hurts us. What hurts us*
> *is the love we are not extending in the*
> *present.*
>
> —Marianne Williamson

In the aftermath of betrayal, you may be hesitant, even highly resistant, to open your heart again. You may need time to be with yourself, process your pain, and receive the support of compassionate friends. This is all natural and healthy.

There comes a time, however, when continuing to focus on your painful story robs you of the joy available here and now. The more you cling to your history, the further you delay your destiny. You need confidence more than sympathy. When the rewards you perceive in opening to a great new relationship outweigh the benefits you perceive in going over old ones, life will deliver your choice.

GIVE IT A REST AND A CHANCE

How do you escape trudging in Miss Havisham's pitiable footsteps? You quit dragging your past lover around with you mentally and emotionally. Perhaps you have seen the hilarious film *Weekend at Bernie's*, in which two guys visit their boss's home and find him dead. Fearing they will be blamed, they prop up his body, adorn him with sunglasses, and carry him through a weekend of hysterical situations. When you carry the corpses of your past relationships into new scenarios, you waste precious time and energy you could use to enjoy a live person. But a dead relationship is in some ways easier to deal with than a live one. Ex-lovers' corpses don't talk back, bother you to process your feelings when you want to watch the big game, or leave their toenail clippings on the coffee table. But they also don't say, "I love you," offer you staggering sex, or stretch your mind with ideas bigger than you have conceived. The Bible tells us, "Let the dead bury the dead." In other words, leave the past to the past. There is just too much life and love available now.

> *If your heart has been broken, let it be broken open.*

Do not breathe life into your victim story by repeating it. Do not use your past as an excuse to not show up in the present and create a better future. It's hard for a new love to penetrate your castle of loneliness if you keep the drawbridge shut with chains of resentment, malice, and self-pity. Life is trying to love you. Are you letting it?

Do your grieving and processing for the time you require, with the help of a friend or counselor. When you feel stronger and ready to connect again, step ahead. Here are some ways to move the process along:

- Perform a release ceremony declaring your completion with your former partner and the misery the relationship and/or breakup entailed.

- Write him or her a letter expressing all of your thoughts and feelings—then burn it.
- Remove and release symbols of the person or relationship that are lingering around your home.
- Do not discuss past relationships when beginning to date someone new.
- Be keen for "victim" phrases that crop up in your conversations. Either eliminate them or reframe them to expressions of empowerment by noting how you have grown as a result.
- Don't speak of your former partner by uncomplimentary names. Strike "Dickhead" or "Wonderbitch" from your vocabulary.
- Find ways to appreciate the positive aspects of the relationship, as well as the elements that made you grow.
- Practice loving yourself to the point that the love you didn't get doesn't matter.

Resentment is like taking some poison and hoping the other person will die. Don't hurt yourself by feeding bitterness or parading your treasured wounds. There are better treasures in store, and you are worthy of their gifts.

WHAT YOU CAN DO ABOUT IT, POINT BY POINT

- Grieve, vent, or process for the time you need, and then move on. If it helps, set a date by which you intend to complete your grieving over the relationship and get on with your life.

- Consider your emotions as currency. The more you invest in the past, the less you have to invest in the present and future. Move your funds to your new account.
- Quit telling your victim story.
- Remove symbols of your ex from your world.
- Do a release ceremony, by yourself or with trusted friends.
- Let appreciation lift you beyond the past and into your present and future.

Too Good to Be True?

—⁓—

"I have struggled through a long string of disappointing relationships," Loretta reported. "I was engaged three times, but never made it to the altar. One guy changed his mind. Another wanted an open marriage. Another died. . . . My track record with men is dismal.

"Six months ago I met a guy I really like. Our connection is awesome—better than any I have ever had. I think we have all the elements of a great relationship, and so does he. But after so many letdowns, meltdowns, and breakdowns, I don't want to get my hopes up.

Things are going so well, they seem too good to be true. What do I do now?"

Some people have experienced so much pain, confusion, frustration, and loss in relationships that when something wonderful comes along, they question it and just wait for the other shoe to drop. But love, harmony, and safety in a partnership seem too good to be true only because they defy a familiar pattern to the contrary. The truth is that good relationships are *good enough* to be true. Through repeated disappointment and observation of poor role models you may have overdeveloped your propensity to endure misery. Now you need to develop your propensity to endure happiness. Then a good relationship will feel like the most natural experience in the world, and anything less will seem weird.

While visiting a poultry farm, a naturalist observed an eagle scratching around in the dirt with the chickens. He asked the farmer, "What's an eagle doing here with these chickens?"

"I found the baby eagle a few months ago when he fell out of his nest," explained the farmer. "So I took him back to the farm and raised him with the chickens. He ate chicken food, slept in the chicken roost, and mingled with the other chickens as his peers. He knows nothing of eagle life, and everything of chicken life, so he thinks he is a chicken and he lives like one. He flies no higher than the top of the roost."

The naturalist, recognizing the eagle's potential, asked the farmer if he could try to help the bird. The farmer agreed, and the naturalist took the eagle to the edge of a high cliff. He held the eagle overlooking the valley and tried to toss him into flight. But the eagle became frightened and clung to the man's arm. Again he attempted to launch the bird, and the eagle held on even tighter.

Finally the naturalist raised the eagle, looked him squarely in the eye, and firmly told him, "I know you have been living like a chicken because that's all you have known and you think you are one. But you are not a chicken—you are an *eagle*. I say you can fly. Your chicken days are over—now fly!"

With that, the naturalist gave the eagle a good shake, and the bird took off into flight. After a few clumsy tries, he discovered the power of his wings, stabilized, and soared. The naturalist smiled as he watched the eagle disappear over the mountains he was born to rule.

The eagle's predicament symbolizes the way many of us have plodded through dating and relationships. We have spent so much time scratching around in the chicken yard, and observed so many others doing so, that we have come to believe that relationships are supposed to be exasperating. Then we settle for less than we really want and wonder why we feel empty. But just because we have accommodated to mediocrity does not mean that is all we can achieve. Like the eagle, we were born to soar higher, freer, and farther.

ACT AS IF

So what do you do when, after dating lots of cocky roosters or clucking hens, an easy-to-be-with bird shows up and you feel disoriented?

1. *Proceed as if you deserve the good that has come your way.* Thank the universe for sending an answer to your prayer. Accept as much happiness as you can, as if you deserve it. Give yourself credit for your courage to persevere through all the frogs you kissed, which led you to the place where you now stand. Keep letting the love in and giving it out.

2. *Don't just sit around watching and waiting for something to go wrong*—like discovering her photo in the yellow pages under "Escort Services"; or his secret wife and five kids showing up at your doorstep; or . . . or . . . or . . . Why hunt for skeletons? If one jumps out at you, deal with it. Until then, enjoy your partner and all he or she has to offer. Besides, you have more meat on your bones than a skeleton, so in any such confrontation you will prevail.

3. *If you have an upset or notice a possible red flag, keep it in perspective.* Don't overanalyze or create a drama that sinks the relationship before it gets out of the harbor. As often as I have seen people miss red flags, I have seen others turn minor incidents into excuses to bail. So what if he gets a call from an old girl-friend? If he tells you he is done with her, take him at his word. If you catch him in bed with her, you can kick his ass on the spot. Until then, give him the benefit of the doubt. "Never trouble trouble 'til trouble troubles you."

4. *Hold the relationship lightly.* The tighter you squeeze or try to control, the less clearly you see, and the more you deny your relationship's natural unfolding. Say to yourself, "If this relationship is good and has substance, it will last and grow in a joyful, healthy way." Love is more about allowing than manipu-lating. Flow and trust will get you what you want far more effectively than worry and forcing.

HOW EASY CAN IT GET?

My friend Sandra spent many years dating through personal ads. She posted and responded to countless notices in newspapers, magazines, and Web sites. Smart, attractive, and successful, Sandra has had a choice of many men to be with, and she can hardly remember all of her dates—and would rather not. She desperately wants her soul mate, but she has not yet found him.

Meanwhile, my friend John lived as a hermit in the remote Halawa Valley on the sleepy isolated Hawaiian island of Molokai. Daily he trekked naked through the jungle cultivating a popular herbal crop. One day John received a surprise visit from his old friend Henry, on vacation from New York, with his traveling companion Lisa. John and Lisa fell in love, got married, and moved to another island, where the couple cultivated a family and (nonherbal) business together.

The contrast between these two stories underscores the power of readiness, willingness, and letting the Law of Attraction take care of the details. Sandra made every effort but got no results, because she was too fussy and enjoyed her independent lifestyle more than she wanted to share it with a mate. (Remember: You can always tell what you believe by what you are getting.) John was simply enjoying his life as he chose it, not particularly trying to find a mate, but not particularly resisting one. Voil'a, an ideal partner showed up at his door with no effort on his part. That's how easy it can be when you are relaxed, open, and in harmony with yourself.

NO PAIN, NO PAIN

Often when I ask friends or clients, "How is your relationship going?" they just sigh and soberly answer, "We are sorting out our issues. A good relationship requires lots of work, you know." Others feel they are somehow cheating if they are not fighting or analyzing their love into jagged little pieces. Others endure unsatisfying relationships until they get sick or die to escape them. Many people have wrestled with relationships for so long that they accept deprivation as a way of life. They keep lowering the bar until it hits them on the head and knocks them out. Then they sleepwalk through relationships and life, living as if all they have is all they can get, while there is much, much more available.

> *Almost the whole world is asleep . . .*
> *Only a few people are awake, and*
> *they live in constant total amazement.*
> —From the film *Joe Versus the Volcano*

Why would sane people participate in insane relationships? Many replicate the model of relationship they observed their parents play out. If their parents fought a lot; drank; jabbed sarcastic barbs at each other; had an on-again, off-again relationship; were emotionally distant, abusive, unaffectionate, sexless, or noncommunicative; or if one parent was absent or unfaithful, the child learns that this is what a relationship is, and, uncorrected, goes on to repeat the pattern. One of my clients reported that his parents could not be in a room together for more than ten minutes without plummeting into a brutal argument. It is no wonder, then, that so many of us equate relationship with work—we grew up in the shadow of relationships that were rooted in hell.

If there is any work to developing and maintaining a relationship, it is dropping the fears and resistance that make it so difficult. Rewarding connection in a relationship is the most natural thing in the world; all else is an anomaly. What hurts is not the relationship, but the beliefs that keep you from enjoying it. When you release the thoughts and attitudes that stand between you and heartfelt connection, you will find all the love you ever sought. Or it will find you.

THE PIVOTAL QUESTION

If relationships are a struggle for you, a good question to ask yourself is: *"How would I be approaching this differently if I were willing to let it be easy?"*

What would you be thinking, saying, and doing if you refused to accept struggle as a fact of relationship life? How would you handle issues if you had greater faith in yourself, your partner, and your process? Where would love guide you that resistance would deny you?

Exercise:
Let It Be Easier

Begin to notice when you start to struggle in your relationship, rather than waiting until you have gotten steeped in it. Become aware of when you clench your jaw, tighten your solar plexus, breathe choppily, and blurt out things you wish you hadn't said. These are your signals to stop right there, take a breath, step back for a moment, and ask yourself if there is an easier way to handle what's going on. Is this amount of fighting necessary? Are you really a victim? Have you assumed malicious intent on the part of someone who may be willing to find a win-win solution? Do you have access to more options or resources than you have been tapping? Are you fighting someone else, or is the fight within you? How would someone who honored him- or herself proceed? The answers to these questions will guide you to a lighter path. You may end up taking the same course of action, but without a sense of resistance. You will be in *action* rather than *reaction*. As a result, you will be far more effective and feel better.

The word "disease" means that you have dissed ease. You have checked out of the flow and into stress. If what you are doing is not working, doing more of it will not work better. The very fact that it is not working is a sign to do something else, or at least think about it differently. Refuse to tolerate struggle, and do not accommodate to situations that demean you. You were not born to play mediocre. You were born to be great. Anything less does not become you.

LESS TRYING, MORE BEING

When a relationship is right and good, it flows naturally. You don't have to spend a ton of time overcoming personality differences, processing childhood traumas, or deciding who is going to pay. You don't have to jump through lots of logistical hoops trying to figure out how be in the same place at the same time. You don't have to sit by your phone or check your voice mail or e-mail every three minutes to see if he has called or written. *People who want to call, do.* People who don't want to call, don't. It's that simple. *No response is a response.* Why would you waste your time waiting for a response from someone who is not responsive? There is far more to dating than waiting.

At this point, less trying will help you more than more trying. Then your dating experiences will be less trying. I know many people who met their partner when they gave up trying. When you relax and feel better, things go better and you become more attractive. Leave horror stories to Hollywood. You have a brighter destiny.

"Good enough to be true" does not mean you meet Prince or Princess Charming and ride off into the sunset together. Even the best relationships have arguments and difficult times. The question is, what is the predominant theme of your being together? Is it mostly stormy, with a few bright moments, or do you basically enjoy each other, punctuated with occasional upsets or challenges? Do you dwell on what is wrong, or can you use your difficulties to grow closer together?

Happiness does not just happen to you; it is something you choose. No matter how long your relationships have been difficult, they can be easier. Either change your situation or change your mind. Or both. Whatever you do, don't accept misery as a fact of life. Why live in a soap opera when you can star in a great love story?

WHAT YOU CAN DO ABOUT IT, POINT BY POINT

- Begin to question your belief that a good relationship is too good to be true. Adopt the maxim "Good enough to be true."

- When a good relationship comes your way, act as if you deserve it and do not question or doubt it.
- If you start to struggle, ask yourself, *"How would I be approaching this differently if I were willing to let it be easy?"*
- Try less, be more.

Why—and Why Not—to Contact Your Ex

—∿—

I dated a woman named Jenny who had a hard time showing up for dates. Although we cared for each other a great deal, whenever we had a date Jenny would arrive hours late, cancel at the last minute, or not show up at all. Her excuse was always the same: she had to take her kids somewhere.

Jenny had gotten divorced a year before I met her, and she was raising two children, ages thirteen and six, by herself. Still emotionally tender from her divorce, Jenny felt guilty about her kids not having a dad at home, and spent most of her leisure time driving them around. Although Jenny wanted to be with me, she feared intimacy and the issues of a new relationship. (She once invited me to her house for a romantic weekend while her kids were at their dad's. When I arrived I was greeted by a friend of Jenny's and her two children, whom Jenny had also invited for the evening . . . so much for romance.)

After a year of trying to make our relationship work, we both realized this was not going to happen, and we tearfully let go.

Over the next six months I thought about Jenny a lot. I recalled the (few) good times we had, missed her, and considered that I had blown my opportunity to be with my mate. Bolstered by my vision, I phoned Jenny and told her I wanted to get together again. She told me that she had been thinking about me a lot, too, and wanted to see me. We made a date for the following Thursday evening.

I spent the week mentally and emotionally preparing to reunite with my love. I was ecstatic to anticipate a new start and possibly a lifelong connection.

At 5:00 PM on Thursday I received a phone call from Jenny. "I have really been looking forward to seeing you," she told me. "But I have to take Tommy to karate, so I don't think I can make it."

Many of us escape into fantasies about the future. Yet we also escape into fantasies about the past. We make up stories about "the way it was" that have very little to do with the way it *really* was. We blow out of proportion the ratio of sparkling moments to painful ones. While future and past fantasies take place at different times in our mind, they serve the same purpose: to offset the pain or lack we perceive in the present by painting a more attractive picture than the one we are living in.

Nostalgia is like a grammar lesson;
you find the present tense, but the
past perfect.
—*Owens Lee Pomeroy*

There is a difference between a fantasy and a vision, between wishful thinking and true guidance. A fantasy offers an avenue of escape from reality, while a vision builds a path to a better reality. A dreamer fantasizes to avoid the unwanted present. A visionary takes steps to replace an undesirable now with a more valuable then.

I have had the propensity to fantasize about several past girlfriends, sometimes years after we were together. As I looked back on those relationships, I recognized mistakes I had made and wished I had hung in there to claim a better relationship. In some cases I contacted my past partner with the intention of rekindling our love. In other cases we remet in uncannily synchronistic ways. (The universe has a knack of getting people together to complete unfinished business.)

No matter how we reconnected, in all cases I ultimately remembered why I was no longer with that person. In some instances my old love had chosen a lifestyle far different from mine, and I realized that we had indeed been heading in different directions. In other instances I remembered the personality traits, communication differences, or lack of chemistry that kept us from forming a lasting bond. In all of these reunions I came to a sense of completion that enabled me to release my fantasy lover and be more open to a real one.

REASONS NOT TO CONTACT YOUR EX

Do not hastily contact your former partner if (1) you are in a relationship; (2) he or she is in a relationship; (3) you have just gone through a painful breakup with someone else; or (4) you have a history of on-again, off-again get-togethers and breakups with this former partner.

If you are in a relationship now, especially one you enjoy, you will kick up lots of issues by reaching out to your past lover, so be prepared. Is it really worth it? Are you following true love, or just fantasizing? Check out where you stand in your current relationship before looking back or outside of it. If you have dissatisfactions or issues with your current partner, face and handle them before looking elsewhere. You may find that when you go deeper with your current partner, you lose your desire to fall back on your earlier relationship. Be sure you are complete with one situation before creating another.

Keep your eye on the road and use your rearview mirror only to avoid trouble.

—*Daniel Meacham*

If your former partner is with someone, respect that. If you really care about your ex, support him in his happiness. If he has found someone with whom he is well matched, let it be. If he is unhappy, however, that is another story. If he is with someone else and he jumps at the chance to get back with you, he has his own lessons and relationship issues to handle.

If you have just broken up with someone (especially if they have left you), your impulse to get back with a previous partner may simply be a rebound reflex. If so, take time to be with yourself and process your breakup before considering calling your past lover. Don't play with your ex's head. Hopping into the sack or having someone hold you when you feel lonely is not worth tattering the soul of someone you care about. If, after a period of time following your current breakup, you still wish to contact your ex, you may be in a better position to do so. But do it out of choice and intention rather than simply clutching at someone to offset your immediate distress.

If you have a history of on-again, off-again drama with your ex, be sure that your desire to connect is not just another act in the same play. If you approach your relationship with the same mind-set you previously had, you will just create the same results. The only way you stand a chance is if one or both of you has changed your attitude in a significant way. Otherwise, don't torture yourself or each other.

CLARIFY YOUR INTENTIONS

Intentions determine results, especially when it comes to a sensitive area like love relationships. Before reaching out to your former partner, do some soul-searching to clarify why you are doing it. Here are some possibilities:

- You are lonely and want companionship.
- You are horny and want sex.
- You feel guilty and want to apologize.
- You just got dumped, your self-esteem is in the toilet, and you want to be bolstered.
- You had a fight with your current partner, and you want someone who was nicer to you.
- You found out your current partner cheated on you, and you want to get back at him or her.
- You are confused and want counseling.

- You are broke and need money.
- You are still mad at your ex and want to continue your argument.
- You value your ex's friendship and want to talk.
- You realize what a great thing you had going and want to get it going again.

Obviously, following most of the above reasons will not advance your quest to create a healthy relationship. But that's not so obvious when you are lonely or hurting. That's why it's wise to do a reality check on your desire to connect, and act only if you feel your motives might be helpful to both you and your former partner.

WHAT YOU MIGHT GAIN BY CONTACTING YOUR EX

Okay, you've run the gauntlet of the above categories and intentions, and the coast seems clear. You phone or e-mail your ex, and he or she agrees to get together with you for a meeting or date. Here are four avenues your reconnection might take, either immediately or over time:

1. You will slip back into your old pattern together and re-create the relationship that left you less than fulfilled.
2. You will remember why you are not together, put your wondering to rest, and get on with your life.
3. One or both of you will speak from your heart, communicate previously unexpressed thoughts and feelings, and you will gain a sense of completion. On

that note you will consciously part with a sense of appreciation.
4. You may renew your relationship and go to a new level.

In scenarios 2, 3, and 4, you will be ahead of where you were when you were wondering, and your reconnection will have served both of you well. In scenario 1, well . . . that's why you are reading this book.

THE LETTER METHOD

If your former partner is now in a committed relationship or does not want to communicate with you, you may do well to write a letter expressing all of your thoughts and feelings. *This letter is for you, not your partner,* although it will help you to imagine her receiving your communication. Tell her everything you want her to know, including all of your thoughts and feelings, for better or worse. Don't hold back anything, and write until there is nothing left unsaid. Simply scribing this letter will leave you feeling immensely free and empowered.

Then either (1) burn the letter; (2) delete it from your computer; or (3) put it aside and forget about it. After a week or two, read it again and see if there is anything you would like to add or subtract. If so, do it. Repeat the process of putting the letter aside, reviewing it, and revising it until you feel whole and good about it.

At this point you may choose to send the letter, but to tell you the truth, I don't recommend it—*unless* the general tone of the letter is loving and supportive of both you and your ex. If you are just repeating what you've already said, going over the same unresolved issues, or laying into your ex, the letter will not advance you. Remember that relationships stay the same unless one or both of you awaken to a new perspective. If you have attained that new perspective and you feel freer, clearer, and more connected to yourself and your partner, your letter or any communication will serve you both well. If not, it's just the same ol', same ol' . . .

If, after thinking long and hard, praying, and meditating, you still feel moved to send your letter or to otherwise communicate, do so. (If, however, your partner has asked you not to communicate with him, respect that.) Just be unattached to the response you may or may not receive. You are writing to express yourself, not to get anything from him. If you have a hidden agenda to rekindle your love; to reinforce your position of being right about your complaints; or to get him to approve or agree, your communication will backfire and you will just have a rerun of the drama that broke you up. If, on the other hand, you can express your truth and simultaneously release the recipient from any particular response, you will bestow your friend with a great gift, along with yourself.

If your intention is for healing, completion, and peace, you will have what you want. If you want to keep fighting or want to manipulate your former partner, *fuggetaboutit*. You have more letting go to do before any communication will bear fruit.

WHEN RECONNECTING MIGHT WORK

Occasionally people reconnect with a past partner and kindle a glorious future. If you have both grown and changed, and you meet with clearer communication and richer willingness, you will find a greater love. Sometimes we need to step back and walk our journey alone for a while before we can give and receive the love we were not ready to handle at an earlier time. When this happens, it's wonderful and you both deserve lots of credit.

More often, however, the desire to get back with someone who has departed is an opportunity to face yourself and show up more fully right where you are. It is not so much the old relationship that you seek, but resolution and moving ahead to claim what you really want now. So in most cases you may simply do better to let sleeping gods lie.

WHAT YOU CAN DO ABOUT IT, POINT BY POINT

- If you are inclined to reach out to a past lover to rekindle your relationship, check out your intentions and tread carefully.
- If you are in a relationship, face and handle your issues with your current partner before considering reaching out to a past one.
- If your past partner has asked you not to communicate with him, respect his request.
- Write your ex a letter expressing all of your thoughts and feelings, and burn it.
- Proceed only if you are free and clean of baggage.

How to Quit Repeating Patterns

~∞~

Georgia's relationships were like a bad reprise of the film *Groundhog Day*: She would meet an attractive guy, start dating, have sex before long, get emotionally involved, and think she had found The One. After a short honeymoon period, her beau would show signs of disappearing. Georgia would grow anxious; then angry; then confront him with her needs. The two would start arguing, and before long he would leave.

Georgia would joke with her friends that she could almost set her clock by how long her relationships lasted. Yet in her heart, she was not laughing, but deeply frustrated. No matter how hard she tried, Georgia just couldn't get a relationship to stick. It seemed as if the same man was showing up every time with a different face. Although each new encounter brought a glimmer of hope, Georgia's love life seemed doomed, and she feared she would never break this distressing cycle.

Repetitious patterns keep recurring only when you do not realize you have something to do with them. You think others or the world are doing it to you, and you seem to have no control over what keeps happening. Men are overbearing; women are flaky; you keep meeting people who lie to you; you can be faithful for just so long; you are a magnet for addictive personalities; your partner violates your boundaries; you fight over money; everything changes after you have sex; you give your power away; you get bored; you marry people before you know them ("I don't date—I just get married"); you let the good ones get away; and on and on and on. . . .

When the pattern continues over time, you may believe you are just unlucky; or you are a victim of unseen forces; or that's just how (men) (women) (relationships) (Scorpios) (you) are. You start to despise the opposite sex or yourself for doing the same stupid things over and over again, and you start Googling monasteries. None of these attitudes or beliefs are helpful, and if you indulge them, you will only dig your predicament deeper. It is not a new relationship you need— God knows, you've tried enough of those. What you really need is to understand your role in the cycle, and break it. Here's how:

1. *Identify the pattern.* For example:

  - You don't set boundaries, but then resent doing things you don't like.
  - You pick people for their looks and then find they don't have substance.
  - You choose men significantly older than you, turn them into a father figure, and they parent you.

- You have sex (less) (more) than you want, and can't get your partner to meet your needs.
- You move in together too soon and feel trapped.

The pattern I experience: _____.

2. *Trace your pattern back to a belief.* Ask yourself, *"What would someone have to believe for this to keep happening?"* For example:

- Men don't stay.
- Women are too demanding.
- I have to prove myself.
- Relationships are more work and struggle than joy.
- I'm the one who has to make an effort to make a relationship work, and my partner just doesn't care that much.
- Partners want more from me than I'm able to give.
- My inadequacies are more real and overwhelming than my strengths.

*What someone would have to believe to keep this pattern going:*_____
_____
_____.

3. *Acknowledge yourself as a powerful creator of your experiences.* You must be very strong, intent, and astute to keep finding the one person at a party who is secretly an alcoholic. Or someone with a good job who will quit the moment they fall in love with you, move in with you, and lean on you to support them. Give yourself credit for knowing how to search out and reel in a

particular personality configuration. If you can do that for a kind of person who doesn't work for you, you can do it for a kind of person who does work. It's time to make the Law of Attraction, which you have worked against yourself, operate in your favor. Affirm:

> *I am powerful to keep attracting certain types*
> *of people and experiences.*
> *I can now attract what I choose.*

4. *Be grateful for the wake-up call.*
Recognizing a self-defeating pattern can be jarring and disheartening, but the only worse course would be to continue it. In most cases a repetitious painful relationship pattern springs from a limiting core belief that is not serving you. (For example: *I am lovable for how I perform, not for who I am.*) Your relationship difficulties have gotten in your face to help you bust the myth you have believed that has kept you small. So challenges are not your enemy, but your friend; appreciating them accelerates moving beyond them.

*How recognizing this pattern can help me:*_____.

5. *Decide if you have really had enough of this pattern and are ready to shift it.*
This pattern has stayed in force because you have perceived some payoff for it. Are you willing to question its value? If you keep meeting unavailable people, for example, you may feel safe not having to get close; if someone showed up who was

actually available, you might head for the hills. When you reach the point where the cost of the pattern exceeds the payoff and you recognize that it hurts more than helps, you are ready to shift. Are you there yet?

*Why I want to shift this pattern:*_____.
*Am I really ready?*_____.

6. *Designate the successful opposite of the pattern.*
Now for the fun: What would your dates or relationships look and feel like if the patterns that have gone wrong went right? Turn your full attention to your ideal scenario and immerse yourself in the vision until you can feel it as real. For example:

- I come home to my lover and I feel safe, secure, loved, and whole.
- We have plenty of time to simply be together, making our day up as we go along.
- We handle money together harmoniously, equitably, joyfully, and creatively.
- Our sex leaves me satisfied and fulfilled physically, emotionally, and spiritually.
- We laugh a lot, play, and enjoy a social life with friends who stimulate both of us.

Actively reinforce your focus with these practices:

- Write the characteristics of your ideal partner and relationship in your journal.

- Write yourself love letters as if they were coming from your enamored lover.
- Create a treasure map with photos or symbols of your ideal partner and relationship.
- Celebrate any sign or indication that you are moving in your desired direction.
- Hold your tongue if you begin to speak or complain about the old pattern.

7. *Seek or create a support system* so that you don't have to go it all alone. There are people out there who are happy to help you, and will.

- Declare your intention to a trusted friend.
- Get into coaching, counseling, or therapy.
- Attend uplifting seminars.
- Use positive affirmations.
- Pray or summon assistance from a higher power.

8. *Take advantage of teachable moments.*
If you start to revert to your old pattern, *seize the moment to consciously make a new choice.* If, for example, you tend to fall into bed with partners too quickly, and you find yourself at a party where someone asks you to go home with him, use the situation to make a new decision that can set you onto a powerful new course. Such crossroads are called "teachable moments," because you can chart a new destiny with one small act, and one healthy choice leads to many more.

"FIRE" THE RELATIONSHIP PARTNERS YOU "HIRE"

On some level you have a matching energy with your relationship partners; something inside you is equivalent to something inside the people you date. When you reprogram the element of yourself that is magnetizing the undesirable behavior, the other person will either change or depart.

> *It's impossible to defeat an enemy*
> *who has an outpost in your head.*
> —Sally Kempton

My coaching client Andy was in a relationship with a woman who constantly criticized, belittled, and demeaned him. As I got to know Andy, I saw that he constantly judged and criticized himself. I told him that he had "hired" this woman and relationship to amplify to a dramatic degree his self-judgments so that he could face them, heal them, and let them go. The essence of Andy's emotional work was not with his partner, but with himself. As a result of this insight, he practiced lightening up on himself and relaxing his mental self-flagellation. Over time, the better he treated himself, the better his girlfriend treated him. In other similar cases, the couple parted because there was no longer an agreement that abuse was acceptable. As Eleanor Roosevelt noted, "no one can make you feel inferior without your consent."

Your relationships are your mirror. If someone is kind to you, he is reflecting your kindness to yourself. If he is cruel to you, he is reflecting self-cruelty. When you realize that your relationship is more about what's going on inside you than what's happening out there, you have identified the source of your experiences, and you can work on your life where it really counts—from inside out.

YOU ATTRACT WHAT YOU RESIST

You always get more of what you pay attention to—even if it is something you dislike. If you have a strong emotional charge against a kind of person or issue, you will not get rid of that situation, but will instead keep attracting it. If, for example, you are hypersensitive about people using you for your money, you will likely keep drawing to you people who use you for your money. The more you resent someone or something, the more it eats away at you. This is where for-giveness can serve as a powerful tool. Forgiveness does not mean that you condone or agree to repeat unhealthy situa-tions, or that you make believe you are okay with a situation when you are not. It means that you withdraw focusing neg-ative attention on a situation so that you demagnetize it and let it go. In so doing, you take back your power from the person or event that disturbs you, and you choose to be happy simply because happiness is a choice. So forgiveness is your gift to yourself. Forgive not because the other person deserves it, but because *you* deserve it.

Think, write, or speak, for example:

[Name], I am ready and willing to let go of whatever has kept our painful pattern in force. I now consciously and lovingly release you from the criticisms and judgments I

have held against you, that we may both be free mentally, emotionally, and spiritually. Likewise, I release myself from the criticisms and judgments I have held against myself. I withdraw my attention from any situations that I have allowed to remove my peace, and reclaim my right to be happy. I bless and release you and myself, and open to all that is good and serves both of us.

Feel free to substitute your own words. It is the sincere intention to release and move on that makes your statement effective and able to create astounding, miraculous results.

APPRECIATION, THE MASTER HEALER

The fastest, easiest, and most effective way to get an unwanted repetitious pattern out of your life is to appreciate it and extract its gift. Practicing appreciation will make more of a difference in your relationships and life than just about any other method.

To release a painful pattern once and for all, be grateful to everyone involved—including yourself—for what you have come to recognize through it. For example, you may try saying to yourself:

- I am worthy of love, and I deserve a partner who is available and wants me.
- I am whole, not broken, and I don't need anyone to fix or save me.
- I do not have to compromise myself to please my partner.

- There must be more to having a relationship than drama, fighting, and hassling.
- Everyone has both positive and negative attributes, and I can draw forth desirable traits by focusing on them.
- Healthy boundaries serve both me and my partner.
- Peace of mind, harmony, and connection are more important than money.
- Sex is more rewarding with someone I care about.
- The messages my family gave me about my deficiencies just aren't true.
- Unconditional caring is more essential than religious, cultural, racial, or ideological differences.

*What I have learned from dealing with my pattern that can contribute to me creating the relationship I desire:*_____.

PERFECT MATCHES, PERFECT TEACHERS

Relationship healing is an inside job. While we have been led to believe that we would be happy if we could just get the other person to change, it is really our mind we need to change to be happy. Your role in creating what you choose is more powerful than you know. *When you accept 100 percent responsibility for your experience, you gain 100 percent of the power to create the experiences you desire.*

Everyone you have ever dated, slept with, appreciated, fought with, loved, hated, married, or divorced, has been a perfect match and a perfect teacher. They came into your life as a learning partner by your invitation, and they exit when you master the lesson for which you invited them. No matter what role they played, they are your loving friend who agreed to help you, as you agreed to help them. Do not resist the good they came to deliver, but appreciate and bless it. When you recognize the perfection in your choices, you are well on your way to making even more perfect choices.

WHAT YOU CAN DO ABOUT IT, POINT BY POINT

- Reframe unhealthy patterns as wake-up calls that motivate you to reach higher.
- Be grateful to everyone who shows up in your love life, whether it's briefly or at length, as a learning partner who ultimately helps you.
- Identify the undesired pattern; pinpoint your belief that keeps attracting it; own your participation in it; extract the lesson it came to deliver; name, claim, and turn your full attention to your desired scenario.
- Regard relationships as your mirror: change yourself and watch your partner(s) and relationships(s) change.
- As you forgive others, you release yourself.

REASON #4.

YOU KEEP FABULOUS PARTNERS AT A DISTANCE.

It's easy to be in realtionship—or say you are—with someone you don't have to deal with on a day-to-day basis. Many peole create ingenious ways to act as if they are in realtionship while holding a part of themselves aside from it. Yet safety is never as rewarding as intimacy, and sooner or later our hunger for connection outweighs our fear of it. If your relationships do not materialize, or they disintegrate before they fulfill you, the following chapters will help you recognize the role you play in lost love, so you can find it.

WHAT YOU CAN DO ABOUT IT

The following chapters will show you how to:

- Evaluate and clarify long-distance and cyber-relationships.
- Understand why someone would be attracted to one-night stands, and replace them with more rewarding partnerships.
- Identify and resolve patterns of keeping "one in the wings."
- Recognize if you or someone you love uses the excuse of being busy as a shield against intimacy, and remedy it.
- Deal with inordinate jealousy in yourself or your partner.
- Keep overanalysis from stifling love.

Close at a Distance

~~~

When Josh met Jackie on an Internet dating service, the two felt instantly drawn to each other. Before long they were spending hours a day sending romantic e-mails and sharing intimate thoughts and feelings.

After several weeks, the two began to speak on the telephone, cultivating their connection. Both felt as if they had possibly met their life partner.

A month later Josh and Jackie decided to meet in person. Jackie flew to Josh's city, where she stayed with a friend and eagerly anticipated lots of quality time with Josh.

Josh and Jackie's first in-person meeting, though somewhat anxious, ended up being sweet and warm. The two stayed up late into the night, continuing their dialogue, Josh tenderly holding Jackie's hand as they spoke.

Then their relationship took an unexpected turn. Somehow Josh became unavailable to spend much time with Jackie.

After a couple of dates, he got busy. He had to work late, attend church meetings, take some alone time, and, it seemed, find any excuse to not get together. He told Jackie that he really liked her and wanted to be with her, but these things just happened to come up. He did not touch her anymore.

After two weeks, Jackie had seen Josh but a handful of times, and even then, briefly. Jackie felt disappointed and confused. What happened to the warm and willing guy she had shared so intimately with on e-mail or the phone?

Jackie decided to confront Josh and ask him how he felt about her, why he had been so unavailable, and if he wanted to continue their relationship. Josh explained that he had feelings for Jackie, but he was not ready for a relationship. He had been divorced a few years earlier, and he was still trying to sort things out.

Although Jackie was disappointed, she felt relieved that she had at least gotten some clarity and direction. The two parted with a polite hug, and Jackie flew home.

A week later, Jackie received a long, intimate e-mail from Josh. The guy she had known before she met him in person was back. Unfortunately, Josh's ability to be present and intimate was limited to far away. He could be close, but only at a distance.

Long-distance relationships, including Internet dating, are slippery animals. For many people, having a lover at a distance is a lot safer than having one at home. The unspoken statement is, "Online or on the phone, I will open my heart to you, reveal the most intimate details of my life, have sex with you, and even fall in love with you. Show up at my door, however, and I don't want to know you. (It's too scary.)"

When I traveled a great deal I met several women who lived

thousands of miles away. That made it easy and convenient for me to not get any more involved than I wanted. If I started to date someone and did not want to continue, I could use distance and logistics as excuses to not get together. But I could have done so if I wanted to. We are all doing exactly what we want to do, and logistics matter far less than intention.

Eventually I began to yearn for a deeper relationship than one based on occasional meetings. I began to date a wonderful woman, Dee, who actually lived near me—what a concept! Dee and I saw each other casually at first, then more regularly. We could get together on the spur of the moment, and didn't need to spend hours on the telephone figuring out (or arguing over) how and when we would meet again. *Revolutionary!* Our relationship developed gradually and organically, with such graceful growth and reward that I finally understood why someone would date a person from the same town. This relationship has borne sweeter fruit than any other, because we were both open, willing, and available.

Long-distance relationships are created and maintained by people who would rather not see each other that often. If this is your choice, that's fine—just be honest about it. Don't make excuses about how busy you are or the timing of things. People who want to get together, do, and people who don't want to get together, don't. It's as simple as that.

It is rare that long-distance relationships survive over time. Because participants either don't want to be together any more than they are; or can't decide if they do; or they want to date others; or they lack the fire of purpose required to burn past obstacles. Not to say that there cannot be real caring or even love at a distance—just not the intimacy of daily life or sexual partnership. (Wild sex one weekend a month is not really an intimate partnership. Titillating, yes. Romantic, yes. Intimate, no.) When you want intimacy more than intrigue or drama, you will have it, and along with it you will have far more reward than distant romance offers you.

Occasionally couples who start out in a long-distance relationship do get together and develop a great relationship. This requires the intention, readiness, and willingness of both partners, and usually needs to happen sooner than later. Otherwise you just have a long, excruciating saga. Or maybe just a life that works for you as you would currently live it.

THE WORLD WIDE BED

Cyber-relationships are generally fraught with thick illusions. It is *really* easy to fantasize about someone you've never met in person. (Is she really a swimsuit model? Did he really go to Paris for business on the weekend?) And it is equally tempting to present yourself as you would like to be rather than as you are. (Do you really still look like the high school graduation photo you sent him? Did Photoshop send you to the gym?) The Internet, with all its technological marvels, has enabled us to wrap longer arms around more fantasy lovers and have deep, ongoing conversations without ever meeting someone in person. And if you want to carry on an affair, the arduous task of sneaking out has been replaced by the simplicity of logging on.

Cyber-lovers or flirtations can certainly be intriguing, but they lack the one element that makes or breaks a real relationship: getting to know your partner, and them you, as real people in the course of daily life. Although you may hold Brad or Angelina in mind, you do not get to listen to his same corny jokes time and again; trip over the dirty jeans he left on the bedroom floor; or wait an hour for her to finish putting on makeup while you are starving for dinner. The person you are live-chatting with may be delightful in many ways, but if you moved in with them you might discover an equal or greater number of annoyances than distress you about your current partner. Only a real relationship will tell the truth about this, not one you filter through a keyboard.

HOW TO MAKE THE MOST OF CYBER-RELATIONSHIPS

Like all calls for love, cyber-relationships offer a fertile opportunity for growth. If you are not already with a partner at home, consider in a cyber-affair:

- How rich and deep can you craft your communication (I don't mean sexy talk) so that you get to know him, and he you, from inside out, with all your humanity as well as your points of attractiveness?
- What would it take for you to get together—not rushed or delayed—so that you could explore a relationship in person?
- Do you really want to get together, or is cyber-dating as intimate as you want to get? Have you been honest with your cyber-partner about this? Has she been honest with you? Would you be willing to go on if you knew you would never meet in person?

If you are already with a partner, consider:

- What do you feel you are lacking in your current partnership that is moving you to seek a cyber-partner?
- Have you confronted your issues with your partner at
  home and attempted to shift the relationship, either
  through dialogue or with the help of a counselor, so
  you can find what you seek where you stand?
- Would you be willing to look at how you are holding
  out in your relationship, apparently to keep yourself
  safe, yet effectively to keep you from having what you
  really want?

BRING IT HOME

The dangers of long-distance or cyber-relationships are not
moral or even logistical—they are emotional. When you settle
for part-time love, you receive part-time fulfillment. In some
cases you do better to get to know someone over time and
across the miles, especially if you need that time and space to
gradually reveal yourself. But if your long-distance relationship or cyber-love becomes a substitute for relationship, it is
not serving you. Whatever you do, don't live a double life. Not
because you shouldn't, but because it hurts. And because you
deserve—and can have—far more than a digital spouse.

WHEN IT WORKS

Friends and clients often ask me if I think Internet dating is
good idea. I tell them that it is as good or bad as any kind of

dating. It's not the form of the connection that matters, but the degree of openness, readiness, and willingness. You can glean the same quality results from conventional dating, speed-dating, computer matchmaking, clubbing, astrological coupling, getting set up by friends, or visiting a fortune-teller or yenta. All of these formats are just venues or excuses for you to do what you want to do anyway. If you sincerely want to meet someone, you could bump into them at Borders; and if you don't meet them there or in other places, you can spend six hours a night online and go on three different dates a weekend, and you will be scratching your head, asking, "Is there anyone out there for me?"

If you do create a good relationship on the Web, it is not because you type sweet or sexy things to your digital honey via e-mail. It is because you spend quality time with her in real life and like her even with the mole on her chin or her spider veins. Love has a way of finding those who seek it, and when you are ready for true closeness, it will not be at a distance.

WHAT YOU CAN DO ABOUT IT, POINT BY POINT

- In a long-distance or cyber-relationship, be honest about your feelings and intentions about whether or not you would like to get together more, or at all.
- Ask yourself: What is the cost and payoff for you to be with someone at a distance? What would be the cost and payoff to be with someone on a daily basis?
- If you are carrying on a cyber-relationship while you are seeing someone else, address your issues, fears,

and purposes with your current partner. Can you go deeper with them?

- What is your heart's desire for a relationship? What would be your next step to have it?

Wanted: Meaningful Overnight Relationship

—∿—

After his divorce, Derrick dated lots of women. In his mid-thirties, attractive, and successful, Derrick was an appealing potential catch. His charisma and sense of humor gave him entrée to many women's hearts—and beds.

When Derrick traveled for his job, he would connect with women in business situations, parties, and singles bars, and seduce them. He did not consider himself a sex addict or a womanizer; he just liked women, and if they were available, he would seize the day. He was honest with his partners and made no promises beyond the moment.

Derrick had a field day for a while, but eventually he began to feel empty. The singles scene got old, and some of the women he slept with were not content with one night of love. They equated sex with relationship and pursued him. Things were getting complicated.

Derrick attempted to continue relationships with some of

his partners, but he just couldn't seem to go the distance. There were too many attractive women out there to settle down with just one. Besides, when women got needy after a couple of dates, he was turned off.

As time went on, the ache in Derrick's heart intensified and he grew cynical. While he badly wanted connection, he found more reasons to keep his emotional distance. Why were there so many women out there, but none who could make him happy?

Derrick was caught between a rock and a heart place. He was an intelligent guy with a lot to offer a woman. Yet his fear of intimacy was as strong as his desire for it, and he could go only so far in a relationship. When the flame was turned up and women wanted more, he would disappear. Derrick was able to confide in several women who became his friends, but he had created two separate categories in his mind: *friend* or *lover*, with no bridge between the two. So the one-night stand became his drug of choice.

Derrick's story could lead to one of several endings:

1. He could go on with his pattern for a long time, perfecting his technique while edifying his emotional walls, growing more disconnected from himself and his partners. Derrick will have a few good female friends with whom he develops intimacy without sex, and a lot of other partners with whom he develops sex without intimacy.

2. Derrick may get someone pregnant or contract a sexually transmitted disease, which moves him to rethink his MO and opt for another path.

3. He may choose a safe, emotionally nonthreatening partner to settle down with, yet crave the passion he felt in his sexual exploits, and possibly engage in flirtations or affairs on the side.

4. Derrick may find someone he truly cares for and take the risk to open his heart. This could be the same woman as choice number 3, but Derrick will have to do the inner work to go to the next level.

A GOOD THING GOING

I saw a bumper sticker proclaiming, "Wanted: Meaningful Overnight Relationship." Quickie encounters are attractive to people in cork-out-of-the-bottle situations, such as those who are just discovering their sexual identity or independence; rebelling against oppressive parents or religion; or getting out of stifling relationships. For others, sexual conquest is a way to validate their attractiveness and worth. Others use impersonal sex as a release or distraction from the stress and pain of their life. Others just like sex and do it whenever possible without attaching meaning to it. For some, it is an addiction. At best, serial promiscuity is an experiment, education, fling, or phase, a reaching out for connection. At worst, it is a pattern that keeps real love and relationship at a distance. You can't have what you really want if you are settling for less.

From the outside, a life of sexual freedom may appear glamorous and enviable. From the inside, it's not so much fun—maybe at first; maybe sometimes; but not in the long run. When I was in college I looked up to one of my professors, a psychologist who sported a long string of hot girlfriends.

Dr. McIntire cruised in a red Porsche convertible, owned a classy pad overlooking the bay, and was on a first-name basis with the maître d' at the Starlight Room—the whole nine yards. While I was sweating it out studying for my finals, he was sweating it out penetrating new territory in multiple orgasm research.

When I became a senior, I traveled with Dr. McIntire and a small group of students to a psychology conference, where I had more personal contact with him than our regular classes afforded. One night after downing a couple of beers together I candidly told Dr. McIntire that I thought he was a pretty cool dude, what with all of his girlfriends. I asked him if he had any advice for me. He set his beer down and gave me intense eye contact (liberated by his mild drunkenness). "Don't be fooled," he told me candidly. "My life isn't what it appears to be."

I was shocked. "How's that?"

"Sure, I have lots of women, sex, and cool stuff," he acknowledged. "But the truth is, I'm a pretty lonely guy."

"You? The original Studly Do-Right? Lonely?"

He smirked. "Sometimes—lots of times—I lie in bed or the bathtub, stare at the ceiling, and feel this huge empty pit in my gut. The women, the car, the apartment create the illusion of filling that emptiness, but they don't really. In some ways they make it emptier."

I just sat there, dazed.

"You have a girlfriend, don't you?" he asked. "I think I've seen you with her on campus."

"That's right."

"She looks like a nice girl. Stick with her. You've got a good thing. My lifestyle has nothing to offer you over what you already have."

With that, the good professor headed for the restroom. But the message had been delivered—in spades. While many people envied Dr. McIntire his sexual exploits, he envied those with a stable relationship. Go figure.

A Quickie Inventory:

(Asked in present tense, but if more appropriate to your past, apply to that time.)

Do you have any or lots of one-night stands?

What has been going on in your life, inside you, that makes them attractive?

What do you enjoy about them?

What do you not enjoy about them?

How much connection do you feel with your partners?

Have you developed rewarding relationships with any of your partners?

Do one-night stands make your life easier or more difficult?

In what way(s) do they help your life?

In what way(s) do they hurt it?

If you had aspects of your relationships or sex life to do differently, what would they be?

Do one-night stands affect anyone besides you and your sexual partner(s)?

What you are really seeking through them?

Are there other ways you might get what you seek?

CONNECTED OR DISCONNECTED?

Sex is a very personal thing. Only you know why you do what you do. (Or maybe you don't.) Nothing is always right, and nothing is always wrong. I am not here to sit in judgment—no one has that right or power. I am here to help you figure out why your love life sucks and to empower you to create relationships that work. Anonymous sex usually contributes to why your love life sucks, and sex with someone you know and like usually helps your love life work. You can do the math.

What you want more than anything else—and if you don't remember anything else from this book but this, you have grasped the most important key—is *connection*. If, after sex, you feel more connected to your partner, yourself, and the people you love and who love you, then it was a very good thing. If, after sex, you feel less connected, it was not such a good thing. We'll address sex more in a later chapter. For now, simply remember to use the connection factor as a rule of thumb for any sexual act, and you will find satisfaction that embraces sex yet goes far beyond it.

WHAT YOU CAN DO ABOUT IT, POINT BY POINT

- Regard one-night stands and impersonal or anonymous sex as a search for connection.
- Notice the feelings that lead you to sleep with someone you don't know, and the feelings you have afterward.
- Notice the feelings you experience when you make love with someone you care about.
- Use your sex life, no matter what form it takes, to get to know and love yourself more.

One in the Wings

—∿—

When Sal met Julie, she was living with another man, with whom she was not happy. Julie professed her love for Sal and swore it was only a matter of time until she moved out of her boyfriend's apartment. Since Sal and Julie lived in cities far apart, Sal decided to back off and love Julie from a distance until she made the move. In the meantime, they spoke on the phone daily and got together for romantic weekends.

One night Sal called Julie on her cell phone, to find that she was having dinner with yet another man. Julie swore their connection was platonic, but Sal sensed otherwise. He confronted Julie and asked her why she was living with one man, professing her love for Sal, and having dinner with someone else.

"I guess you've discovered my pattern," Julie admitted. "I always like to have one in the wings."

People who stockpile romantic partners or potential partners are insecure. Fearing they are not lovable or attractive, they collect people who make them feel safe and wanted. They do not trust that they will be able to maintain one happy relationship, so they line up numerous partners to make sure they will always have one in case they need it. In our last chapter we focused on serial one-night-standers; here we will look at serial—actually, *overlapping*—romantics.

Although queuing lovers offers comfort to an unconfident psyche, the plan is ultimately self-defeating. If you do not love or value yourself, you can never collect enough people to prove your worth. If you do love yourself, you do not need anyone else to prove it.

A thousand half-loves must be forsaken to take a whole heart home.

—*Rumi*

You cannot go very far or deep with one person if you are carrying others in your back pocket. A line of future partners is good insurance against getting too close to one—and is a sure sign of resistance to intimacy. You further complicate your life by having to do a lot of plate spinning to keep your partners from finding out about one another. Or if they do know about one another, you have to keep each of them feeling important enough to hang in there.

There are two ways to keep love in the baby pool rather

than the ocean: (1) simultaneously string along several partners who are also satisfied with shallow relationships; (2)
create a long series of brief relationships that self-destruct
before they go anywhere. Both plans meet the goal of staying
romantically and/or sexually stimulated, but ultimately they
crash and burn because you can't run fast or far enough to
escape yourself. Even as you discuss Camus by candlelight or
lick chocolate off each other's chests, you will feel hungry for
more sustenance than candlelight or chocolate alone can
deliver. Wholehearted presence nourishes, where symbols of
romance leave wanting.

WHAT DO YOU REALLY WANT?

Dating lots of people can be fun and exciting. If you are just
launching into dating, or you have just broken up or gotten
divorced, you are wise to explore all possibilities and keep your
options open. There is a time for checking out partners and a
time for going deeper with one. Be honest with yourself and
your partners about which phase you are in. Wherever you
stand in your journey, authenticity will get you more mileage
than manipulation. Consider these important questions:

- Are your dating decisions motivated by joy, or fear?
  Security, or insecurity?
- Is your current date or relationship someone you
  could and would go deeper with, or are you just filling
  space or buffering yourself from getting hurt?
- Are other possible partners real possibilities, or just
  carbon copies of the situation you now find yourself in?

- If you were totally honest with yourself and your partner(s), what would you be saying or doing differently?
- How would you feel about focusing on someone you really like and letting the others go?

These are not easy questions to answer. Yet your responses will illuminate a direction that skirting them will cloak. Now you must face the question that has terrified you into keeping one or many partners in the wings: *Do you believe that you can find deep, rich love with one person by simply being yourself?* While emotional nudity can seem terrifying, it's the only way to prove that you are lovable for all of you, not just the parts you are willing to show. Trusting your innate worth will carry you much further than micromanaging to keep partners in your court.

If you are dating someone who has one or many partners in the wings, you have to decide what you value in a relationship. Are you okay with them flirting or sleeping with several people, or would you prefer to go deeper with them exclusively? If you, too, are maintaining a bullpen, you have a matching energy, which will keep the relationship going as it is until one of you shifts or hits an emotional wall and disappears. If you are ready to go deeper, let your partner know. If not, tell the truth.

MORE IN THE WINGS

The expression "one in the wings" is a misnomer, because those who keep one in the wings rarely keep just one in the wings. Usually there are several—or many—in the wings.

While attending a conference, I was assigned to be a room-mate with another fellow. During our week together Toby and I became friends. One night I noticed him writing a check imprinted with his name and the names of two women, all with the same last name. "Are they your wife and daughter?" I inquired.

"No, those are my two wives," he explained.

"Are you a Mormon?" I had to ask.

"No, I just have two wives—not on paper, but by mutual agreement. I was married to one woman and I met another. We all liked each other, so my first wife agreed to let me take another wife. I had a child with the second woman, and we are all raising her together. We all get along quite nicely."

Well, all righty then.

The next evening I was on the telephone for a while, and Toby asked me if I would mind completing my call so that he could make an urgent one. When I hung up, I asked him, "Do you need to call your wives?"

"No," he answered, "I need to call my girlfriend."

Within the next year Toby divorced both of his wives to marry his girlfriend. I guess he just liked to get married. His property settlement must have been a fascinating pie to slice.

If you are dissatisfied where you stand, you are not likely to find satisfaction by switching partners or accumulating them. You master relationships by recognizing and magnifying the value of what you have. Sometimes when you shine the light of gratitude on your current relationship, you and your partner will know that your relationship is over, and you will end it with honesty, integrity, and kindness. Sometimes you will fall in love all over again and wonder why you ever thought about leaving. Neither of these scenarios is the same as searching for or finding someone better—or in Toby's case, an additional partner.

One great rule of thumb for all relationships—and all of life—is:

Appreciate what you have before asking for more.

Sincere appreciation helps you find more of what you value right where you stand. Or it will move you on to the next phase or level. In either case, appreciation will be a worthier guide to your next step than escape or resistance, or the accumulation of playing pieces that keep going in circles on the game board, with no one winning.

DO YOU CRAVE MORE INTIMACY?

We have used the word "intimacy" quite a lot, and you will continue to find it here as a consistent theme. When most people hear the word, they immediately associate it with sex. That's because for most people, the only intimacy they experience is with a sexual partner. Yet there is so much more to intimacy than sex! The word "intimacy" can be broken down into three smaller words that reveal how to create it: "into me see." It may be scary to admit your more vulnerable feelings, but if you can find the courage to speak them, you will grow a relationship stronger than you ever could with multiple shallow partners. A good relationship cannot only stand the truth; it is *built* on the truth.

> *The easiest kind of relationship is*
> *with ten thousand people; the*
> *hardest is with one.*
>
> *—Joan Baez*

Love can feel scary if you believe that full truth will reveal things about you that you would rather not have anyone else see or know. Yet showing all of you is the very ticket that will take you to the connection you crave. Having one or many partners in the wings can feel comforting if you fear that your current partner will bail. But in keeping other lovers in your back pocket, *you* are bailing. Yet there is so much more to you than the one who wants to bail, or the traits you fear exposed. True intimacy will not send a partner running away from you— it will send a partner running to you.

WHAT YOU CAN DO ABOUT IT, POINT BY POINT

- There is a time to explore being with different people, and a time to focus on just one. Where do you stand on the continuum?
- Consider if you are stockpiling romantic partners, and why.
- Regard keeping one or more partners in the wings as a trust and confidence issue. Do you believe you can have one great relationship? Why or why not?
- Appreciate, savor, and draw the best from what you have before seeking more.
- Create intimacy by letting your dates or partner see into you more.

Taming the Green-Eyed Monster

—✺—

Ted and Lauren, a couple in their forties, attended one of my full-week seminars. They had been married about a year, and each had been married at least once previously.

At the seminar Lauren was threatened by Ted's interaction with other women, and she became intensely jealous. The ensuing upset between the couple spilled into the group process, and everyone was aware of Lauren's anger. The irony of the situation was that Ted was quite innocent in his interactions with the women; he was friendly and kind, but not flirtatious, and had nothing going on with any of the women. It was obvious to the group that Ted was a devoted husband and wanted his marriage to work. By contrast, Lauren's fear was running her; she admitted that she had had major jealousy issues in her previous relationships, which tattered them.

One evening Lauren had a meltdown, and the couple brought their issue to the seminar session, where group members attempted to help Lauren deal with her jealousy. One woman poignantly noted to Lauren, "Wouldn't it be a shame if you finally met a man who was trustworthy, but lost him because you did not trust him?"

Lauren left the seminar early, and within a year the couple divorced. Ted remarried a few years later and began a family.

There is a fable about a man who went to visit a friend who lived in the country. During the night, the visitor awakened to go to the bathroom and mistakenly found his way to a storage room. When he opened the door, he looked down to see a large poisonous snake coiled up at his feet, ready to strike.

The next morning the host opened the storage room door to find his guest dead on the floor. At his feet was a large coiled rope. The visitor had mistaken the rope for a snake and died not of snakebite, but a heart attack. The snake did not kill him—fear did. Yet he was just as dead as if a poisonous serpent had bitten him.

> *Illusions are as strong in their effects*
> *as the truth.*
> —A Course in Miracles

Events and circumstances do not ruin relationships. Fear does. Fear causes us to see things that are not there, and react to them as if they are. Then we develop massive defense systems against the object of our resistance, attack it, and allow it to run our lives. If we do not question our beliefs and seek the true source of our upset, we become like Don Quixote, fighting windmills as if they were dragons. Thus we embue windmills with the power to slay—and they do.

SOCIAL INSECURITY

Jealousy, that dragon which slays love under the pretence of keeping it alive
—*Havelock Ellis*

Jealousy is an expression of insecurity. People who know their worth and feel safe in their relationship do not worry about their partner leaving or being stolen, or go to lengths to prevent that from occurring. Nor do they attract partners who are tempted to stray. Secure people recognize that a healthy relationship is impervious to predators, and they relax in the confidence that they are enough to fulfill their partner. If their partner does not recognize this, that is their problem. If they are easily led elsewhere, they are not worth trying to hold on to anyway.

Ted and Lauren's breakup was the result of a self-fulfilling fear. Lauren doted on Ted's "infidelity" to the point that she pushed him away and ran away. She could have handled her upset more maturely by trusting in his love and dedication to her, or by examining her fear with a counselor or therapist. Many people feel jealous, a little or a lot, but do not allow the feeling to undermine their relationship. If feelings of jealousy are detracting from your relationship, there are unhealthy and healthy ways to deal with it.

Unhealthy Ways to Deal with Jealousy:

- Seethe with resentment and say nothing.
- Seethe with resentment and make sarcastic remarks.
- Assume a victim position and wonder why this is happening to poor you again.
- Criticize and attack your partner.
- Criticize and attack the person you are jealous of, and tell them to stay away or else . . .
- Run away from your relationship.
- Have a fling or affair to get back at him or her.
- Withhold sex, attention, or communication as a punishment.

Healthy Ways to Deal with Jealousy:

1. Face your feelings and try to understand where they are coming from.

- Do you believe you are not good enough for your partner?
- Is fear of loss a theme in your life?
- Do you not trust (men) or (women)?
- Have you been burned by a past partner?
- Did one or both of your parents show you a model of someone who could not be trusted?
- Have you been unfaithful in this relationship or a previous one?
- Are you attracted to other people, and you are projecting onto your partner your desire to be with someone else?

2. *Voice your feelings to your partner*—not to control or punish your partner or start a fight, but to invite them to walk with you beyond your discomfort. Simply saying, "I notice I feel jealous when I see you talking at length with Susan," may open a door to a dialogue that will draw you and your partner closer. If you can express your concerns without attacking your partner, you may find that the feelings dissipate and you can get on with your relationship without jealousy standing between you.

3. *Address your jealousy with a counselor or therapist.* If your jealousy is an ongoing issue that colors your relationships, you may do well to enlist the help of a good counselor who can help you get to the root of your upset and reprogram your distress in favor of greater trust and self-confidence.

4. *Pray or request help from your higher power.* If you feel helpless, you can summon help from the power of your Creator, by whatever name you know It and however you personally relate to It. Many people receive answers to prayers for healed or improved relationships, help that makes a huge difference in the long run.

IF YOUR PARTNER GETS JEALOUS

*My wife's jealousy is getting
ridiculous. The other day she looked at
my calendar and wanted to know who
May was.*

—*Rodney Dangerfield*

A jealous partner offers both of you an opportunity to grow. Jealousy, like all unpleasant emotions, is a call for love. Your partner has forgotten for the moment that you love or care about him, and he needs to be reminded—not by pandering to jealous demands or by guiltily or apologetically defending yourself, but by looking him in the eye and sincerely telling him, "I care about you and want to be with you. You need not to be concerned about me and _____. I am with you." Making one good, honest statement of your feelings is your role. Receiving the message is your partner's role. If you are sincere and he cannot hear you, he has work to do. Be patient, but do not indulge undue processing. If you do not share his focus on the jealousy, you empower him to move beyond it.

The above scenario is the cleanest one. There are variations on the scene that call for a different approach. If you are indeed interested in someone else, this requires a different conversation (see below). If you have a pattern of attracting jealous partners, you need to look at why you are attracting them. Does a jealous partner make you feel wanted and important? Do you have one foot in the relationship and one foot out? Is the drama of processing jealousy attractive to you? Are you putting out signals to other people that your partner is picking up?

While there are many variations on the theme, and potential responses, you can use jealousy, like all relationship upsets, as a justification to push each other apart or to come closer. You will reap the fruits of your intention.

If you are with a partner who is unduly jealous, do not take her upset personally, and do not assume it is your job to fix her upset. It is your job to rest in the truth. Give your partner space to feel and communicate her feelings, affirm your love for her, and support her to find ways to feel better in her own way and timing. Meanwhile, stay peaceful yourself. If your partner has even a small intention to move beyond the upset, she will find a way to do it.

IF YOU OR YOUR PARTNER IS INTERESTED IN SOMEONE ELSE

This chapter is primarily focused on undue jealousy. If you or your partner is indeed attracted to someone else and acting on it through fantasy, flirtation, or affair, it's time to be more honest with yourself and your partner. What do you find attractive about this other person that you are not finding in your present relationship? Do you have any unspoken upsets or disappointments you need to communicate? Are you happy with yourself and your life? Is your relationship getting too intimate for you, and you would rather bail than go deeper? Would you rather not be with your partner? Or do you truly care about your partner and want to be with him, but you have allowed fear or resistance to cloud your appreciation and attraction?

These questions may be difficult to answer, but they lead to many treasures. Sincere answers can improve a relationship with potential or get you out of a bad one. They can also undo a pattern of moving from partner to partner without finding gold with any of them. Great relationships rarely just drop in your lap. They are built by opening your mind and heart and trusting truth to take you where you want to go.

THE MONSTER'S HIDDEN GIFT

Feelings of jealousy offer you a powerful opportunity to reprogram old mental and emotional tapes that have probably run you for a long time. Now you can use them as a fulcrum to practice confidence in yourself, your partner, and your relationship. Jealous feelings are less about people and events, and more about mistrust, lack of self-worth, and fear. Rather than casting guilt onto your partner, address your own issues. Refuse to let jealousy dominate you. With practice, you will recognize that you are bigger than any negative feelings that come up. Why waste time fearing or hating when you can enjoy the love you seek and deserve?

Every relationship experience is an opportunity to grow closer, and the experience of jealousy is among the most fertile of these opportunities. The stronger the feelings that arise, the greater the invitation to find more depth and meaning in your togetherness. No third party has the power to undermine a good relationship. Build your relationship from the heart out, and both of you will be safe and your relationship whole.

WHAT YOU CAN DO ABOUT IT, POINT BY POINT

- Use jealousy not as an excuse to attack or argue, but to practice self-worth and confidence in your partner and relationship and to grow closer together.
- If you are habitually jealous, try to get to the core of your upset either through introspection or with your partner or a counselor.
- Review the list of unhealthy and healthy ways to deal with jealousy, and upgrade your approach.
- If your partner is jealous, regard her upset as a call for love. Do not pander to demands, but communicate your truth and caring for her.
- If you or your partner is interested in someone else, use the experience to shed light on your relationship and improve it.

Analysis Paralysis

—⁓—

Ben is a brilliant man who holds advanced degrees from several highly respected universities. He understands quantum physics, rebuilt his auto engine by himself, and can debate the subtle differences between the philosophies of Camus and Sartre.

When it comes to relationships, Ben has had a harder time. Since he has lived most of his life in his head, Ben has analyzed his romances to death. Whenever Ben let a woman close to him—which was rare—he would see her through his mind, not his heart, and he would process every experience to oblivion. Since most of the women Ben met wanted love more than intellect, he could not manage to get a relationship to stick.

Ben was married once, to someone who participated at length with him in analyzing their feelings. He and his wife spent a lot of time arguing and dissecting their relationship, to the point that they were wrestling with issues far more than they were enjoying each other. Eventually they divorced.

Yet Ben's thinkaholism was no accident. His father had left his family when Ben was a child, and the wound was too much to bear. So he took refuge in academia, a safe fortress in a threatening world.

When Ben attended one of my seminars, he got in touch with the feelings he had submerged over many years. He acknowledged his pain and anger over his father's departure, his frustration over his dismal relationships, and his loneliness. I watched in awe as the man's wall of self-protection cracked and burst. At the end of the program, Ben noted, "This week I took the biggest step of my life. It was just eighteen inches—I moved from my head to my heart."

A year later I received a photo of Ben and his fiancée. Ben looked youthful and bright, and he was smiling. On the back of the photo Ben inscribed: "You can't think your way to love."

In Herman Hesse's classic book *Steppenwolf*, miserable Harry Steppenwolf discovers the mystical Magic Theater. On its door he finds a striking notice: "Price of Admission: Your Mind." If you want to find or reclaim magic in your relationships, the same entrance fee is required.

We live in a culture that both celebrates love and teaches us how to avoid it. Intellectual prowess enables us to travel to the moon, search eight billion Web pages in .29 seconds, and converse with people on the other side of the world while walking to lunch. Yet what good is all of this if our hearts are still aching for love?

> *Real love is a pilgrimage. It happens*
> *when there is no strategy, but it is*
> *very rare because most people are*
> *strategists.*
> —Anita Brookner

The mind makes a fantastic servant but a lousy master. It was intended to enhance the quality of our life, not suppress it. Analysis is appropriate in many domains, but in the realm of relationships it must take a second seat to the heart. If you intend to plumb the depths of love, you must go beyond thinking and offer your full presence while receiving that of your partner. Whatever enhances your presence is a gift to you and your partner. Whatever detracts from your full presence is a curse. In every moment of your relationship, you are choosing between the two.

WHAT TO DO IF YOU OVERANALYZE

- Consider how much time you spend processing, analyzing, or dissecting your relationship, either by yourself or with your partner.
- Ask yourself if this MO is bringing you the joy, connection, and love you seek. Recognize that, to the contrary, it is distancing you from what you really want.
- Practice getting in touch with your feelings and receiving the messages they offer you. Are you angry? Hurt?

Lonely? Attracted? Sexually stimulated? There is no such thing as a bad feeling. Every feeling brings you a gift and a message. Emotion is *e-motion*—energy in motion. Where are your emotions guiding you to move?

- Consider coaching, counseling, or seminar(s) with a guide who can help you connect with your heart and live more from it.
- Communicate your feelings and your experience to your partner, and invite him or her to do the same.
- Cut your computer time.
- Engage in a physical activity daily—yoga, workout, swimming, gardening—that will get you into your body and ground you.
- Learn and practice some form of meditation that will help you quiet your mind and tap in to clear inner knowing.
- Play, laugh, rest, and engage in self-nurturing activities that reduce stress and deliver ease.

WHAT TO DO IF YOUR PARTNER OVERANALYZES

- Encourage your partner to do some or all of the above.
- When he goes into overanalysis mode, don't go there with him. Stay in your heart and your experience, and express your feelings rather than your analysis of them.
- Communicate directly: "I really love it when we can just be together and enjoy our relationship without analyzing it. Can we just have some more fun?" End of message. Do not use this statement as a springboard to figure out why.

- When your partner goes into processing, gently massage her shoulders or back.
- Invite your partner to share physical activities with you—walking, hiking, yoga, swimming, dance, love-making.
- Laugh, play, and get silly.
- Get away from the processing zone and take care of yourself. Take a walk, listen to music, do your hobby, or visit a friend.
- Cut out the above section and tape it over your partner's computer monitor. Add a smiley face to soften the message.

WHAT TO DO IF YOU BOTH OVERANALYZE

- All of the above.
- Less talk, more sex.
- Create an agreed-upon word or signal you can use to break the cycle when you get into it. For example, "I think we're doing it again," or a finger pointing to your head. Agree that when one of you does this, you will both stop and take a twenty-minute break. During the break, each go to your separate space and do something relaxing or distracting from your processing. During this period you will likely receive insights that will move you to either not continue or short-circuit your processing so that you can get on with real life.
- Share regular physical and self-nurturing activities together, as listed above. Add simultaneous massage to the list.

- Meditate or pray together.
- Attend heart-centered seminars—not those that are analytical—together.
- Write lists of what you appreciate about each other, and read them aloud to each other.
- Read the poetry of Rumi, Hafiz, and Kabir together.
- Remember the good feelings that brought you together.

THE PERFECT MARRIAGE

Alchemists speak of the "mystical marriage," which is not between two people, but between two elements of yourself. You embody both the inner man, representing reason and intellect, and the inner woman, representing passion and emotion. Whether you are physically a woman or a man, both components are significant, and your quest for a soul mate is really the quest for balance and harmony between your inner male and inner female.

A great master I studied with explained it thus: "The head alone is a tyrant, and the heart alone creates chaos. The marriage of the two is mastery." If you tend to live in your head, you seek the balance of its soul mate, the heart. If your life is ruled by your emotions, you seek reason and wisdom for balance.

Real therapy is losing your mind and coming to your senses.

—Dr. Fritz Perls

Apply analysis when appropriate, but keep it on a short leash when joy beckons. Like tiny blades of grass that eventually overturn paved concrete, give love the slightest opening, and it will dismantle your walls against it. You will not figure your relationship out, so don't even try. Just follow your instincts and show up as much as you can. Your head thinks, and your heart feels. Combined, the two make a gorgeous couple.

WHAT YOU CAN DO ABOUT IT, POINT BY POINT

- Quit trying to figure out your love life, and allow your feelings and instincts to guide you.
- Put a lid on long, cyclical analytical discussions, and cultivate connection rather than dissection.
- Step away from the computer and engage in activities that ground you and get you into your body.
- Share nonanalytical, physical activities with your partner. Get outside, get massages, make love, and laugh more.
- Cultivate the marriage of your inner male and inner female to attract or deepen your partnership with a mate.

REASON #5.

YOU DON'T CAPITALIZE ON KEY TURNING POINTS.

The choices you make at relationship crossroads make all the difference in how the relationship turns out. If you miss a key opening or overlook a signal that the relationship is going nowhere, you will land in the wrong port and wonder why. Yes, you will get more chances in later relationships, but if you recognize significant moments of choice and work them to your advantage, you can and will have what you want—sooner rather than later.

WHAT YOU CAN DO ABOUT IT

The following chapters will show you how to:

- Pivot on unsuccessful dates or relationships to correct your course and get what you want next time.
- Attract the kind of partners you desire and avoid those you do not.
- Formulate and distinguish between your "required" list and your "preferred" list.
- Deal with changes in your partner or yourself.
- Make rejection work in your favor.
- Make the best of partners who are "almost it" but still "not it."

This Can't Be It

My last relationship before I met Dee was tumultuous. My partner and I spent long hours probing and arguing, punctuated with brief intervals of joy and appreciation. With drama as the prevalent theme, we fought, vented, wept, hung up the phone on each other, called back, broke up, and got back together again. Then the unfulfilling cycle started all over. I had never experienced such insanity. Eventually the turbulence adversely affected my work and friendships.

Not wanting to be a quitter, I tried to hang in there to make the relationship work. But it got worse. I asked the universe for a sign as to whether to stay or leave, and although I received numerous indications to leave, I stayed anyway. Things got weirder and weirder until there was no question in my mind that I needed to go. Finally I cut the cord.

At that point I threw up my hands and shouted to God, "If this is what a relationship is, count me out!" I decided that if I couldn't enjoy a harmonious, rewarding partnership, I would just go it alone. And I would have.

Then I met Dee. She was recently divorced and not looking for a repeat performance either. As we slowly, cautiously began to spend time together, I was amazed by the absence of drama in our relationship. We actually had a good time with each other—what a novel concept! Our dates were easy, fun, and uplifting, and I went home feeling whole and peaceful—a radical reversal of the pattern with my previous girlfriend.

Over time, I realized that a relationship could be a blessing in my life rather than a problem. I also recognized how my previous relationship had amplified my desire for a drama-free connection. By contrast, it showed me what I did not want and led me to discover and create what I truly valued.

All relationship experiences fall into one of two categories: *It* or *Not It*. *It* moments and relationships feel rewarding and empowering, like you are coming home to where you truly belong. *Not It* experiences feel like you are fighting to survive in a land foreign to your soul; they drag you down and leave you feeling small, alone, and disempowered.

One of the best realizations you can come to in the aftermath of a painful experience is, *"This can't be it."* If you really mean that, you are far ahead of where you were when you started. Distressing as the experience may have been, it has led you to the question that will point your way to higher ground: *"If this can't be it, what is it?"*

Contrast is a masterful mentor. If a crazy, painful, or self-destructive relationship leaves you no longer willing to tolerate mean-spiritedness or insanity, it has served you well.

Rather then regretting the experience, pivot on it and make it your ally by asking, "If that was hell, what would be heaven?"

Don't waste any time or energy cursing the jerks you've lived to tell about. In retrospect you will recognize them as friends who assisted you to discover and take your next step. Once they have fulfilled their purpose, they can exit stage left (and often do). Then you will honor that relationship as a crucial motivator to escape from dating hell.

WHAT TO QUIT

In the aftermath of a bad experience, you may be tempted to quit relationships. That is not necessary (or possible). What you need to quit is the kind of relationship that hurts, or the pieces of a relationship that hurt. Don't head for the monastery because you had a bad experience—or many. Instead, use them as springboards to where you would rather go. Step back for a time if you need to, but don't hide in a hole and justify your isolation by identifying your ex as the source of your agony. The source of agony is stinking thinking. The source of ecstasy is expansive thinking. The quality of your life depends less on what happens to you, and more on what you think about it.

Exercise: From "Not It" to "It"

Record what would happen if what went wrong in the past would go right in the future.

In a past or recent painful relationship:
In my next or desired relationship:

What I didn't like about my partner:
What I seek to like about my partner:

What I didn't like about the relationship:
What I seek to like about the relationship:

What I didn't like about myself:
What I seek to like about myself:

A good relationship is not the reward for your suffering, but the natural result of what you learned from it. The only purpose of pain is to teach you to avoid situations that may lead to more pain. Then your relationships and life become an ever-richer expression of the greater *It* you want and deserve.

DEAL BREAKERS

Before you plunge into dating or mate seeking again, do this exercise:

Exercise: Required and Preferred

Take a sheet of paper and write two headings side by side:

Required   **Preferred**

Under "Required," record the traits of your desired partner or relationship that are nonnegotiable. If your partner doesn't embody any one of these traits, you are not even going to consider this person or make any effort to explore a relationship with them. For example:

Required

1. Honest
2. Passionate to be with me
3. Financially stable
4. No addictions
5. Available

Under "Preferred" list attributes that you would like in a partner or relationship, but would not be deal breakers if they were not present. They are the icing on the cake; if someone did not possess these traits, you could still enjoy being with him or her. For example:

Preferred

1. Tall
2. Enjoys nature
3. Good sense of humor
4. Pet lover
5. Likes to dance

Now comes the most important part: when you meet or date a possible relationship partner, stay true to your list. If you discover this person drinks heavily, for example, stop there. Remember that your list of deal breakers was developed as a result of painful or unsuccessful experiences from your past, so why go there again? How many times will you pay to watch the same bad movie?

Dater's Advisory: You will probably be tested. Let's say you have had a pattern of going after people who are hung up on their ex-partner to the extent that they are not able to be fully present with you. So you add, "Can show up and have a good time without turning a date into a therapy session" to your "Required" list. Soon you are off on a date with someone promising, but when dessert arrives it triggers in him sad memories of his last breakup. Before you know it, you are in the middle of a saga that makes the *Star Wars* series seem like a sitcom by comparison. This is the universe's way of seeing if you really mean business about getting on with your life. It's time to bid this contestant *ciao*. If you can say no when it counts, you will break the old pattern, and that *This Can't Be It* element will no longer be an impediment in your dating journey.

Your "Preferred" list will help you if you tend to be too picky. If you are prone to dis people for minor flaws, this list will help you keep your relationship in perspective. You will also be tested here. Okay, so he does not do a mean salsa. Or she doesn't quite understand fuel injection. It's not the end of the world. You like this person for who she is and how you feel with her, and your life is better for the time you are with her. This could be more important than his left-footedness, and there is more to relationships than discussing Sunday's NASCAR winner. Don't miss the gold because it comes in an unexpected wrapper.

All experiences, including dating, fall into two categories: those in which you grow in joy, and those you learn from through challenge. Even the best relationships include elements of both. Joyful experiences lift your heart. The more difficult experiences help you learn not to repeat them. If you get the message and make a new choice next time, you win big. So don't curse the bummers; they serve a purpose. Thank your discomfort for motivating you to seek better, and then go about the business of turning your stumbling blocks into stepping-stones. There is a gift in it all.

Could you keep your heart in wonder at the daily miracles of your life, your pain would not seem less wondrous than your joy.

—*Kahlil Gibran*

WHAT YOU CAN DO ABOUT IT, POINT BY POINT

- Appreciate the *Not It* experiences for helping point you toward *It* and propelling you to get there.
- Don't curse the jerks for wasting your time. Instead, bless them for motivating you to move ahead.
- You don't need to quit dating or relationships because you had a bad experience. Use the experience to fine-tune and eliminate the parts that didn't work so that you'll be ready for the next time around.
- Make a "Required" and "Preferred" list and stick to it.
- Every dating experience falls into two categories: (1) to be enjoyed; and (2) to be learned from. Find the gift in both.

Shift Happens

———

During the first evening of a two-night couples seminar, a fellow named Gregg stood and made a public profession of love to his girlfriend. Gregg poetically acknowledged how much he appreciated her and their relationship, and declared that he was ready to open his heart to her as his beloved. Gregg's soliloquy was so touching that it left most of the audience in tears.

The next evening Gregg showed up at the seminar alone. "Where is your girlfriend?" I asked him.

"She broke up with me today," he answered soberly. "Do you have any idea why?"

I sure do. Gregg was ready to go the next level, and his girlfriend wasn't. So she got scared and split. Just as relationship beginnings are governed by matching energy, relationships are maintained by it and end when it no longer exists. Every couple subconsciously agrees to connect at a certain level of intimacy. As long as both partners remain at that level, the relationship thrives. If one of the partners goes deeper and more serious (or shallower and less serious), the other partner must either match that person or depart.

The good news, I told Gregg, was that there was no true loss to him. He was now ready for a deeper, clearer relationship, and the strong energetic signal he was putting out would attract a partner who was ready, willing, and available to meet him there. Perhaps his girlfriend would think about it and decide to join him. Or maybe he would meet someone else. It didn't really matter. Gregg had done his part, and the Law of Attraction would orchestrate the logistics to follow.

DRIFT HAPPENS

Gregg's shift was quick and unmistakable. Many couples drift apart over a longer time. They simply grow in different directions. Or one partner changes and the other doesn't. Each day they disengage a tiny bit, until one morning they wake up and realize "we aren't the people we used to be, and we really don't know each other anymore." It is quite disconcerting to look into the eyes of someone to whom you once felt deeply connected but now do not recognize. Yet the dilemma offers a powerful opportunity for truth telling. If you can be honest about what you feel, you will generate movement. You might grow closer together or you might part. In either case you will be better off than making believe there is a match where there is not, trying to squeeze a dead past into the living present.

If you, your relationship, or your partner has shifted or drifted, you may be tempted to deal with your pain and disorientation in one of several ways:

1. *You continue to play your role but fade away inside.* You smile, put on a pleasant front for your partner and neighbors, and do your best to look happy. Meanwhile the lights are on but nobody's home. Your mind, heart, and spirit are elsewhere, and your relationship is little more than a movie set with no building behind the facade.

2. *You distract yourself and lead separate lives.* You become a workaholic; spend lots of time with your friends away from home; grab a joint or drink the minute you get home; watch TV or sit at the computer for many hours a day; shop with a vengeance; flirt with people at work; or have affairs—all so that you don't have to feel your uncomfortable feelings or deal with the issues of your relationship.

3. *You try to stay the person you were in order to avoid conflict.* When you attempt to be someone you are not, you only frustrate yourself and disconnect from your partner more. Good relationships honor and encourage both partners' authenticity. If someone changes, accept where you both are and let your relationship be big enough to handle the changes. If your relationship has substance, you may be pleasantly surprised at the gifts your authentic expression brings. If

the relationship does not have the substance, you may have outgrown it.

4. *You try to force your partner to shift.* This only creates more tension and frustration. You can't pull the petals of a flower open before they are ready. Everything has a right timing. In an environment of care and support, both partners will grow at the maximal rate. Demand or pressure is not a form of love, but one of fear. Love is the great healer and transformer.

HEALTHY RELATIONSHIPS ARE EMPOWERED BY CHANGE

A woman who had been married for forty years told me, "My husband and I have had at least four marriages within our marriage," meaning that they each grew to new levels, remet, and reinvented their relationship that many times. And their love grew only deeper. Love is not a static thing; it is always evolving to greater breadth and depth. If you are not regenerating, you are degenerating.

If shift has happened in you or your partner, trust and celebrate it. It is a sign of life, and you are in a far better position than those who have settled for stability at the expense of passion. It is more important that you live true to yourself than that you lock either of you into a mold. Yes, change can be scary in that sometimes when couples change they end up parting. And yes, it can be exciting in that other times when couples change they become even more alive, together or apart. Trust is key, here, as always.

Never try to force someone to stay or go. Find comfort in knowing that if you are real about who you are and what you want, you will attract a person who meets you there. Sometimes that may be your current partner and sometimes it may be another person. Don't put a face on love. Don't manipulate love. Just love, and love will take care of the details. Gregg's profession of love was not the end of his life—it was the beginning.

WHAT YOU CAN DO ABOUT IT, POINT BY POINT

- Be clear and confident about who you are and what you want in relationship. Let your words and act be aligned with your true intentions.
- Be sensitive to signals that you may have drifted from your original connection, and if so, do what you can to restore life to you and your partner.
- If change happens in your relationship, let it be for the best.
- Never try to force someone to stay or go.

Dialing in Dates

—⁓—

After dating Chuck for too long, Toni decided she had had it with men who couldn't be fully present. After their final frustrating date, Toni vowed to herself, "I refuse to see unavailable men anymore."

A few months later Toni was shopping in a mall with her preteen son. Suddenly the boy tugged on her sleeve and asked, "Mom, why aren't you talking to Chuck?"

Surprised, Toni asked her son, "What are you talking about?"

"Chuck has been standing right next to you talking to you for a couple of minutes," the boy explained, "and you have been ignoring him."

Toni shifted her gaze and, sure enough, Chuck stood just a few feet from her. During the entire time he had been trying to get her attention, she hadn't even seen him.

Toni was not ignoring Chuck; she simply did not notice him. When Toni refused to see unavailable men anymore, she wasn't kidding. Without even trying, Toni had screened Chuck—and men like him—out of her field of vision. We all see what we want to see, and do not see what we do not want to see.

We think in secret,
and it comes to pass.
Environment is our looking glass.

—James Allen

Your intentions and expectations are like electromagnets that draw people and events into your experience. Everyone else will not show up on your radar screen. This is why you keep meeting certain kinds of people, and will never meet others. If you want to change the kind of people you meet (or increase the likelihood of meeting the kind you like), the place to start is right where everything else in your life starts—your head.

A gay man who attended one of my seminars explained, "Several years ago my lover was killed in an auto accident. I felt devastated and told a few friends, 'I don't know if I can go on living without him.' A few months later I was diagnosed with AIDS, cancer, and leukemia. Yow, did my words come back to greet me!

"I began doing lots of soul-searching, and realized that I really did want to live. I began to speak life-affirming words again and engage in life-affirming activities. I have felt better and better, and I just came from the doctor, who gave me a clean bill of health."

Such is our power to shift our experience by consciously

focusing our thoughts. Focusing on possibilities yields you access to more possibilities, while focusing on limits shows you more limits. My friend Hannah has built her wealth through a booming entrepreneurial business. She loves to make money and move it around, and she is one of the most expansive thinkers I know. Hannah learned of a contest in which Oprah Winfrey was choosing a small group of women to attend a private four-day seminar presented by Oprah and experts who appear on her show. Most of the women were to be chosen on the basis of essays they wrote, and a few were to be chosen at random. Hannah did not think she would write a winning essay, so she simply submitted her name for the random drawing. A month later she received a phone call informing her that she was one of the four women chosen. Surprise—but not really.

In the Bible we are told, "To him that hath, more shall be given, and to him that hath not, more shall be taken away." This tenet would seem quite unfair, as it affirms why the rich get richer and the poor get poorer. But the passage is not biased; it simply illuminates a universal principle of mind: whatever you think about, you get more of.

You cannot have your mental radio dial set on WBUMMER and receive shows on WAWESOME. If your needle is stuck on the dial, you could have a different date every night for a year, and you would just keep meeting the same ol', same ol'. Different heads on the same puppet. Old prison, new paint job. New actors reading the same script. Insanity is doing the same thing in the same way and expecting a different result.

If you are tired of the same playlist and wish to reset your tuner:

Don't:

- Keep complaining about the dates and relationships that haven't worked.
- Explain to new dating partners why your marriage(s) failed.
- Label yourself with a particular dysfunction.
- Find people to agree with you about your predicament and complaints.
- Keep arguing with people you don't get along with.
- Indulge in movies, TV shows, novels, and tabloids glamorizing painful or disastrous dates and relationships.
- Enter social situations where most people do not match your interests or goals.
- Participate in groups that keep beating a victim drum.
- Indulge in inner mental chatter about what's wrong with you or your partners or relationships.

Do:

- Think and talk about your ideal partner and relationship.
- Give yourself the benefit of the doubt when assessing the path you have taken that has brought you to where you now stand.
- Thank your dates and partners for the positive gifts they have bestowed upon you.
- Make a "treasure map" of your desired situation by pasting photos and headlines on a poster board you will see often in your home.
- Spend a few minutes each day visualizing a mental

movie of your perfect relationship, to the point that you get the feeling of having it.

- Be selective about movies and books that focus on positive outcomes.
- Participate in groups, meetings, and social occasions where people are aligned with your interests and positive outcomes.
- Talk to new dates about your desired possibilities.

RELATIONSHIP PASSWORDS

Just as you need a password to access important files on your computer, you need certain mental and emotional codes to move to the next level of dating and relationships:

1. *Intention*: When you really mean business and you want what you want more than what you have been getting, your pattern will change. Toni had to get fed up with absentee dates before she resolved to improve the quality of her dating partners. But when she did, she really did. When your intention is strong, so will be your results.

2. *Self-worth*: Know that you deserve enjoyable dates and a great relationship. When you recognize your immense beauty and the unique gifts you have to offer a lucky partner, the game shifts from "Will I ever find someone without camel breath?" to "Who out there is worth receiving what I can give?" If you want someone to fall in love with you, fall in love

with yourself first, and you will be utterly irresistible. (To develop self-appreciation, write yourself a love letter from an ideal lover who desires, respects, and appreciates you for all of your great qualities.)

3. *Openness*: Allow your good to flow to you. Suspend your beliefs about what can't happen or what could go wrong, and be a willing receiver. Children laugh three hundred times a day, while adults laugh only fifteen times per day. What do children know that adults have forgotten? They live in a realm where anything is possible, and life is a big game with all kinds of presents waiting to be opened. We would all do well to return to that openness to magic.

CHOOSE YOUR MODELS

One powerful way to amplify your signal is to focus your attention on people who model relationships that work. When I coach someone having relationship trouble, I ask them, "Can you think of people in your life who have good relationships?" Usually they take a while to answer, and sometimes they cannot come up with even one response. That's because they have been fixated on relationship problems, and thus limit their range of vision and resulting experience. I advise such clients to keep their antennae up for people who are enjoying each other—they are out there, for sure. The more you do this, I explain, the more you increase your chances of becoming one of them.

Your point of attention is your point of attraction. If you want to know what's coming next, examine what you are focusing on now. Even if you know just one or a few couples who are truly enjoying each other, think about them more than the others. Regard them as real, and the others as aberrations. Befriend people you respect, and spend time with them. Laser in on the good they demonstrate, and that good will soon belong to you.

RESENTMENT NAILS YOUR COFFIN

Just as surely as celebrating models of what you want increases your chances of getting it, envy and resentment push it away from you. Never begrudge or criticize those who have what you wish you had, for in so doing you distance yourself from your good. "They probably fight behind closed doors," you snippily think or say. "I'll bet he's cheating on her." "Did you see that ugly dress she wore? She obviously gained a few pounds." To *belittle* is to "be little." If you are stuck in a little world, it is because you keep thinking little thoughts. Your salvation is bigness—big visions, big hopes, big appreciation, big generosity, and big respect for those who offer you an example that what you want is possible.

Resentment and backbiting are emotional suicide. They bring you no reward and only dig your grave deeper. If you observe someone getting something you want, go there with him. Bless him, congratulate him, and thank him for showing you that you can have it, too. You will never get what you want by cursing those who have it. They have it not instead of you, but as a signal that you are coming closer to having the same good for yourself. Curse them and you curse yourself, for you drink from the same size cup you offer your neighbor. Allow others their happiness, and you will surely be next.

Who ends up with a great relationship and who keeps missing the boat are no accidents; the process is as scientific as water boiling at a certain temperature and freezing at another. While your dates and relationships may seem random, chaotic, or uncontrollable, you have a big say in how your dates and life turn out. You may be just steps away from connecting with someone who matches you in wonderful ways. A small tweak on your mental tuner can open you to a world you thought was unavailable. Who knows, the person you seek may be standing just a few feet from you, and you needed just a small tug on your sleeve to look up and see him or her.

WHAT YOU CAN DO ABOUT IT, POINT BY POINT

- Recognize the relationship between the thoughts and feelings you dwell on and the partners who show up in your life.
- Accept responsibility for the relationships you have attracted.
- Shift the range of partners to which you have access by pulling the plug on conversations and attitudes that reinforce what is not working, and instead indulging in words and attitudes that point you toward desired results.
- Develop your intention, self-worth, and openness as passwords that allow you access to your desired dating pool.

- Focus on role models of individuals and couples who inspire you and demonstrate that the relationship you want is possible and available.
- Drop any form of resentment or backbiting toward successful couples. Make them your allies by celebrating their good as a harbinger of yours.

Rejection Is Protection

—⁓—

Seminar Participant Julie: I have been dating a guy for about six months. He is a single father, divorced for about a year, and devoted to his six-year-old daughter, whom he cares for on weekends. He has been really nice to me, and I would like to have a committed relationship with him. Last week he told me that our relationship couldn't go any further, because his daughter is not ready for a new mother. The girl doesn't like me (I don't know if she would like anyone), and he can't deal with the stress of trying to bring a new woman into his house with an unhappy child. I feel heartbroken.

Alan: Rejection is protection. While this fellow is a devoted father, he is not ready for a relationship. Or he is hiding behind his daughter to disguise his own choice not to be with you. In either case, you are being protected from being with someone who is not prepared for a relationship with you. You deserve

someone who is available to show up and let you into his life. Let go of trying to force a relationship with this man, and make space for someone who can meet you with a whole heart.

It hurts when someone you care about doesn't want you, or leaves. Yet in the midst of your tears or anger it's difficult to see the overall path of your life. If someone leaves you by surprise, rejects you for an odd reason, or makes a lame excuse, let her go. Don't stew over your loss. Instead, celebrate that you are being saved from a bad situation. She was not suited for you, and she is clearing space for something better. This takes faith to recognize during a dark moment, but I assure you it is so. Take heart.

A powerful relationship lesson came to me in a dream. I dreamed that a friend of mine had just gone through a painful breakup with her boyfriend. She felt devastated because she had thought for sure this fellow was her soul mate and they would be together for life. Now she was heartbroken and feared to face her future.

In the dream I was telephoning my friend from two years ahead in the future. From that vantage point I knew what had happened since her breakup; her future was already history to me. During that time she had met a wonderful man, they had married, and she was very happy. The breakup was of no consequence now; in fact, it put her in a position to meet this fine fellow.

On the telephone I told her, "Please listen to me. I know this sounds crazy, but I am seeing your life from two years ahead of where you are now. I know what will happen, because from where I am standing it has already happened. Within the next two years you will meet an awesome man and be happily married. You've got to believe me."

If you are in pain, loss, or confusion, you've got to believe me, too. Your breakup is not the end of your life. It may be the beginning.

WORK WITH THE WILLING

The motto "work with the willing" has been a supreme guiding principle in my work and relationships. When someone is willing, everything works. When someone is unwilling, nothing works. Doors open for the willing that are closed to those with weaker intention. Willingness can propel you beyond huge obstacles, while lack of it will stop you at the tiniest bump in the road. Willingness is a far more significant factor in any decision than most people recognize; as you understand and respect its role, you will find relationships that half-heartedness would deny.

A man convinced against his will is
of the same opinion still.
—*Bert Winn*

Many people, when dealing with an unwilling partner, go to great lengths to make them willing. They try to seduce, psychoanalyze, inspire, motivate, manipulate, control, threaten, force, argue, and stand on their head in a hundred different ways to get them to say yes. Most of the time such efforts are wasted; you would have been better off just asking the person

if he was willing or not. If he says no, hems and haws, or
reaches for excuses, you have your answer. Go no further. The
thing you would like to have happen with this person is not
going to happen with him. It's time to seek your good through
another avenue.

Others say they are willing when they are not. Words are
the least part of communication; energy and action speak far
more truthfully. People can lie with words, but not with their
life. What they do and how they live makes a stronger statement than what they say. Do not depend on someone's statement of willingness alone. Observe his or her deeds. The
bigger the talk, the smaller the action. You can always gauge
intentions by results.

---

*What you are stands over you the
while, and thunders so that I cannot
hear what you say to the contrary.*

—*Emerson*

Your strongest power to attract someone who is willing is to
be willing yourself. Rather than trying to make others willing,
contact the part of you that is willing, and live from that. The
strength of your intention will serve as a beacon for those who
want to meet you there, and will weed out those who don't.
This will save you long, agonizing wrestling matches with
dates and partners who are sort of there but not really, and give
you access to people who want to show up as much as you do.

DON'T TAKE IT PERSONALLY

If someone bolts by surprise or for a lame reason, their departure may not be about you. They may be afraid or have issues you don't understand or can't control. We live in a culture that harbors many illusions and dysfunctions in the domain of relationships, and many people do unreasonable things that a clear-thinking, openhearted person would not. There are a million reasons why people run from love, none of which are valid. People do things that seem reasonable to them in a moment of fear but make no sense when held up to the light. So don't use their exit as an excuse to punish yourself. Thank God you received a sign or answer before the relationship went any further. There are healthier people and ways to get what you want.

If someone leaves for a reason you respect and understand, trust that this, too, is in your highest good. What seems like a tragedy in a given moment can turn out to be a gift in the big picture. The less you fuss and resist, the wider you open the door for a great partner to arrive at the right time and perhaps in an unexpected way. Destiny is extremely clever! It recognizes your intentions and finds ways to deliver it. In the meantime, find wholeness within you independent of passing events.

WHEN TO TAKE IT PERSONALLY

If partners keep leaving you for the same reason, or your relationships keep turning out the same way, take it personally. An important lesson is calling to you. When you extract the gift it seeks to bestow, the situation will serve no further purpose and will disappear. If you are doing something that is pushing people away or undermining your intentions, recognizing it is the first step to grow beyond it. At such a point your best move is to face yourself rather than just continuing to pick new partners. Wake-up calls are as productive as they are jarring.

Your starting point begins with one question: *Is there a theme that keeps cropping up, a particular sentence that people tell you when they leave?* Do they tell you that you are too needy? Can they not handle your temper tantrums? Can they not get a commitment out of you, even something as simple as what you want to do the next night? These are just a few examples. Step back for a moment and try to be unbiased. Why do you think people don't stick with you? Could there be a grain of truth in what they say?

Do not use people rejecting you, even one, as an excuse to beat yourself up. Use it as an excuse to find value in yourself, and hope. With some fine-tuning you can have a great relationship. I have seen people who, after many years of tanked relationships and feeling hopeless, blossom and find a perfect partner. You are not lost—you are exploring. Rather than resisting your process, embrace it, and let your experiences, even the painful ones, lead you where you want to go.

THE PROTECTION YOU OFFER

Just as someone is protecting you by leaving a relationship that isn't working, if you leave someone you do not want to be with, you are protecting him. If you don't feel passion for your partner or relationship, you are not helping him by staying. Although it may be painful to say good-bye, you are clearing the way for him to find someone who really wants to be there. While breakups usually kick up distress and disappointment, ultimately reasons make themselves known.

Do not, however, broadcast to your partner that you are doing her a favor as you are walking out the door. The last thing someone who is getting dumped wants to hear is that you are doing it for her own good. Even if this is true, she probably feels vulnerable or upset, so tread lightly. Later, when the dust settles, the story will make more sense to both of you, and you can look at angles you could not see during the storm of a breakup. For now, simple honesty and kindness are your best allies.

Neither lean on the principle I've just described to justify rash or reactive departures. If you have thought significantly about ending your relationship, meditated and prayed about it, and deeply considered the well-being of both you and your partner, and you still feel that it's best to leave, then trust that your decision will ultimately serve both of you. If, however, you are exiting because you are afraid, angry, or in heat because some hottie has turned your head, you will create more confusion than you are trying to solve, and you will have to return to your original crossroads and choose again more wisely.

TWO WAYS TO CHANGE YOUR LIFE

The mother of excess is not joy but joylessness.

—*Nietzsche*

Rejection or the end of a relationship is not the worst thing that can happen to you. Interpreting events against yourself is. There are two ways you can change your life: (1) *change people and circumstances in your environment*, and (2) *change your mind*. Sometimes you can change your circumstances, but you can always change your mind. If someone leaves you, there may be nothing you can do about his choice. But you can still love, accept, and appreciate yourself; relax into the possibility that all is well; and regroup to attract someone better. I recommend plan 2, which will bring you far more relief far more quickly and place you in the optimal position to attract the person who is waiting just on the outside of the door through which the last person exited.

WHAT YOU CAN DO ABOUT IT, POINT BY POINT

- If someone leaves you, consider that your path is being cleared for something better.
- Work with the willing.
- Don't take rejection personally. It's often not about you.
- If people keep leaving you for the same reason, regard the wake-up call as a gift and use the data for your growth.
- You protect others by leaving when you don't belong with them.
- While you cannot control the actions of others, you can choose how you look at events and interpret in your favor.

Almost There

—∾∾—

Cindy dated Kerry for about six months and liked just about everything about him. She would have easily married him if it were not for one big problem: Kerry was a severe workaholic. He left for work early in the morning and came home after 7:00 PM each night. On weekends he brought his work home, and their dinners at romantic restaurants were regularly interrupted by cell phone calls.

Cindy expressed her deep affection for Kerry, as well as her upsets about the amount he worked. He told her that he understood her feelings, but this was just a crucial time at work and there were a lot of projects to be handled.

Cindy decided to adopt a "watch and see" attitude, in hopes that Kerry would be more present with her. Yet over the months, nothing much changed, and she was just as frustrated after month six as she was after month two.

Finally Cindy reluctantly admitted to herself that Kerry had just so much space on his disk for a relationship, a far cry from

her vision of connection. After she bid Kerry farewell, she wondered, "How could I get so close and yet be so far?"

If you find yourself with someone who has many of the traits you seek in a partner, but you cannot get together with them because they are not available or they have a deal-breaker characteristic or situation, regard them as a *representation*. A representation is someone who is not your ultimate partner, but who shows you that (1) you know what you want; (2) there are people out there who embody the qualities you value; and (3) you must be getting closer to having it. While you may be inclined to stomp away mad and curse life for playing with your head, you will advance more rapidly by regarding such a person as a harbinger of good things to come rather than as ammunition for frustration.

JUST ONE MORE TWEAK

Relationships are more a process than a goal. You are constantly rethinking and refining who and what you want in a relationship and setting yourself up for new and better results. No matter how short, long, weird, or wonderful a relationship is, when it ends you have a better idea of what you want, and your next date or relationship choice will reflect your upgraded criteria. Even a single date can be a turning point in your refinement of your choices.

In the aftermath of being with someone you wanted but could not have, your next move is to add the missing trait to your list of requirements for a partner. In Cindy's situation above, for example, she would add "He works a sane amount and has time to be together" to her list. Then she would keep her antenna up for people without cell phones surgically implanted in their ears, and without home offices or long commutes. The clearer she is about what she wants, the faster and easier she will recognize and attract it.

Be not dismayed if you get tantalizingly close to what you seek and miss it by a hair. Instead, get excited—you are near indeed! Irish engineer C. Y. O'Connor rose to national prominence in late-nineteenth-century Australia when he constructed a 330-mile water pipeline from Perth to Kalgoorlie. Many people criticized O'Connor for his outlandish scheme, and, like many great inventors, he became a laughingstock. When the pipeline was completed, the big opening day came, and thousands eagerly awaited the flow of water. To O'Connor's great disappointment, the pipeline spurted just a few drops. The next day, sadly, O'Connor committed suicide. A few days later the water gushed profusely. If the inventor had waited just a bit longer, he would have seen the realization of his dream.

You may also be that close to your relationship dream coming true. A few drops of water may not signal the failure of your efforts, but instead may be a prelude to it. Bless your partial manifestation, and it will lead to a whole one.

PLENTY OF CHANCES

One of the most seductive relationship illusions is the belief that you missed your one big opportunity to be with the right person. Now you are bereft, doomed to wander vagrantly along the Boulevard of Broken Dreams because you were too stupid to recognize a good thing and you blew your big chance when you had it.

If this sounds pathetic, it is. Although Hollywood and your nervous relatives would have you believe there is but One for you, and if you miss The One, you will have missed it all, their vision is warped and deserves no indulgence. "Chances" are not by chance at all. Opportunities show up in direct proportion to your willingness to recognize and capitalize on them. You can make anything out of anything, so why not make it what you want?

When you are ripe, ready, and willing to receive a great partner into your life, he or she will show up without a lot of handwringing or gymnastics on your part. If someone appears but does not ultimately fill the bill, if you are truly ready someone even better will show up. It's not about statistics, crossed stars, or luck. The magic is in you.

RITUALS

Many people engage in elaborate rituals to put them over the edge to draw Mr. or Ms. Right into their life. They light candles; write or speak affirmations; pray; consult psychics and astrologers; create treasure maps; join dating services; hire matchmakers; buy new lingerie; enlist voodoo practitioners; and (go figure) read books like this.

All of these steps can and do work for many. If you understand *why* they work, you will get better results and shorten your journey. Rituals and techniques work because they help build two key ingredients that bring any goal to life: *belief* and *intention*. If you have both, you can't lose. Even if you have a lot of one and a little of the other, you can get your toe over the goal line. If both are weak, you will continue to wander through the wilderness, a.k.a. dating hell. When you voice an affirmation or build your treasure map, for example, you are establishing a mental and emotional matrix of the relationship you seek. You are immersing yourself in the idea and energy of your goal, which increases your power to attract it. When you reach a certain threshold of belief and intention, the universe will help with the logistics. If there is something you need to do to connect with a partner, you will know it and it will be fun. If not, just relax and be yourself, and he or she will find you. I have seen this principle succeed thousands of times, and it will work for you if you use it.

Now for the Cliff Notes version: You don't have to do any of this stuff. You just have to be open and willing, and be sure that your resistance does not choke out your desire. But—ah, here's the rub—if you have not been getting desired results, you may need to do something proactive (phooey, I hoped I could make it through the book without using that word) to raise your energy to a more productive frequency. That's where rituals, consultants, and books like this come in. They help you line up with your vision rather than your history. Then you have an open field before you. When you finally put points on the board, recognize that the techniques themselves didn't do it for you—you did it for yourself with their help.

DEVIL OR ANGEL?

When your relationship with Mr. or Ms. Almost Right ends, you might find yourself judging him or her as a devil for enticing you and not coming through. Yet that person is more of an angel. The word "angel" means "messenger." The person with whom you almost had a relationship has delivered a crucial message to you: *There are people out there who can make you happy. Don't give up. Keep going until you have what you want.*

Rather than throwing darts at Mr. or Ms. Almost It Who Didn't Come Through, draw a little halo around that person's head and kiss him or her good-bye with love. Be proud of yourself for getting clearer on the kind of partner you want. Okay, so this last one was still in love with his mother, or she had a shopping addiction; there are others out there *without* disqualifying habits, and now you have your radar set for them.

If it almost happened, you were almost ready. That's really good. Now just keep getting ready until you are really ready. Your experience with your representation may have just put you over the top and set you up for someone you can wrap your arms around who will stay.

WHAT YOU CAN DO ABOUT IT, POINT BY POINT

- Do not curse "almost it" relationships, but celebrate them as representations that you are close to your goal.
- When you have identified an undesirable or deal-breaker trait in a potential partner, pivot on it and tweak your list so that you head toward its desirable opposite in your next relationship.
- Relationship "chances" increase in proportion to your willingness and readiness to recognize them.

- You can use rituals to speed up the process of connecting with your partner. Just recognize that the magic is in you, not the ritual.
- Regard Mr. or Ms. Almost Right not as a devil, but as a harbinger of good things to come.

REASON #6.

YOU SETTLE FOR SCRAPS AND MISS THE BANQUET.

Once you have a relationship going, there are many levels of reward you can experience. Many people settle for less than what they really want, and can have. Some get into patterns that keep stress to a maximum and joy to a minimum. Yet no habit is so deeply rutted that you cannot extricate yourself from it and forge a new pathway that works for both you and your partner.

WHAT YOU CAN DO ABOUT IT

The following chapters will show you how to:
- Stabilize or stop an on-again, off-again relationship.
- Create a sexual relationship that fulfills you on every level.
- Move beyond a "fight-then-sex" pattern.
- Allow one partner to make healthy choices for the partnership when the other partner is not in a strong position to do so.

On-Again, Off-Again . . . Stop!

Three months after Andi fell in love with Tom, she moved in with him. It didn't take long before their romantic bubble popped and morphed into conflict. Emotionally distraught, Tom came to me for counseling. I encouraged him to hang in there and do his best to move beyond the challenges facing the new couple.

Over time, the relationship drove Tom more and more crazy. Both partners had addictive personalities that fueled their clashes. Finally Tom confessed, "I can't take this anymore. Andi and I have decided to break up." Sounds wise to me, I told him.

A month later Andi invited Tom to get together to finish communicating so that they could both move on with their lives. The next morning Tom phoned me and reported, "I had the most wonderful evening with Andi. We connected so strongly that we ended up making love. Now I realize how much I miss her, so she will be moving back in with me." Recognizing that Tom had made up his mind, I told him I was glad he was feeling better about being with Andi, and I wished him well.

You can guess what happened after that: Tom and Andi enjoyed a month of bliss before their issues blew up in their face again. The next day Tom was in my office, pacing back and forth, complaining that this was not a healthy relationship and he needed to get out. I told him that frankly I agreed, and I would like to see him in a more rewarding situation.

A month later Tom and Andi were on again, then off, then on, then off. This torturous pattern went on for three years. Even though the chemistry between Tom and Andi was basically toxic, nothing I said could convince him to break it off. The stars in his eyes obscured the scars in his heart. So I just tried my best to support him in whatever decision he was currently making.

Finally Tom decided to move across the country to put distance between himself and this destructive relationship. True to form, Andi phoned him after his move and invited him back. But this time Tom's "no" was resolute.

Later that year Tom met a woman with whom he created a much saner and more stable relationship, which has grown and deepened over the years.

On-again, off-again relationships are exasperating. They usually drag on for years, with neither partner feeling fulfilled. Such couples toggle between massive blowups and passionate reunions and are never sure if they have a future or just a past. In the meantime, they miss the present. Matching unresolved issues interlock, and they are more difficult to disengage than mating or fighting dogs. Sometimes you can't tell the difference.

As a friend or observer, you may offer sincere, wise advice to steer your friend(s) in a better direction. But unless one or both of them are willing to listen, your suggestions will fall on deaf ears. Usually both members of such a couple are quite stubborn, and (though they would not admit it) they enjoy the drama. So after you have spoken your piece, back off and let them figure it out. Eventually they will—the hard way, perhaps, but if that is how they need to do it, that is how they need to do it.

THE FEAR FACTOR

If you are in an on-again, off-again relationship, you may be putting up with pain and frustration because you are afraid of losing something only this person can offer you. Maybe it's great sex, or financial security, or you have a public image you want to maintain. Meanwhile you don't realize how far you've drifted from the happiness you seek. Or if you do, you don't recognize how you are contributing to the drama. Perhaps you believe that relationships are supposed to be brutal and that it takes years of hard work and struggle to arrive at peace. Or that any kind of attention is better than no attention. Or you are addicted to adrenaline and require a certain amount of stimulation to feel alive. Or you fear intimacy, and stay at war to avoid it. Or you equate intimacy with war. Or . . .

If you are stuck on a seemingly never-ending rollercoaster, you need to admit a few things:

1. Despite occasional moments of bliss, this relationship is not healthy or working.

2. You deserve more than warfare or spending half
    your time deciding whether or not you are going to
    be together.
3. You are contributing to the drama by participating
    in it.
4. You have the right and power to make a clear choice
    that will shift this pattern.
5. A better relationship awaits you if you are willing to
    claim it.

In counseling with Tom, he revealed the fears that were
keeping him stuck: He was getting older, and he did not think
he was as attractive as he used to be. Andi was younger, sexy,
and charismatic; Tom imagined that if he lost her, he would
never find someone else so desirable who would love him. He
felt flattered to be with such a radiant woman and proud to be
seen with her. Andi, too, had her issues: she was driven by a
sense of inadequacy. She came from a dysfunctional family
with an abusive and emotionally absent alcoholic father. In
Tom she sought a sense of stability and security that she had
missed in her childhood and previous relationships. If Tom
left, where would she be?

Tom and Andi's scenario illustrates that your problem is not
your disturbing partner or even the relationship; it is fear and
lack of self-respect. Thus your route to freedom is mapped in
your answers to these crucial questions:

• What fear is behind keeping the unhappy game going?
• If you were not afraid, what would you be doing
  differently?

- If you knew you were worth a healthy partnership, how would you proceed?
- How would someone who loved him- or herself be handling this differently?

If your relationship choices are motivated by fear of losing, you have already lost. Your partnership is a far cry from the true purpose of relationship, which is to bestow joy, creativity, connection, and celebration. When you act from strength rather than self-protection, you will remember who you were before you let inadequacy call the shots. Then your path will be clear and your results will shift. If your relationship is going to change, it is going to have to change inside you first. If you wait for your partner to do the work, you are depending on luck. If *you* take the step, you are proceeding from smarts.

YOUR PASSIONATE PRESENCE

Some on-again, off-again relationships are not particularly stormy—just familiar, convenient, and boring. Both of you have settled into a passionless rut. You date each other for a while, then don't, then date each other for a while, then don't, and on and on like that. Or you lead separate lives, try each other for a while, and then retreat to your respective scenes. This might be a healthy practice if both of you were joyful in your life and joyful when together, but most scenarios like this are dangerously low on life force. Both partners have lots going on inside their heads and hearts that they do not share or act upon. So you have two people showing up in a ghostly way; the relationship is not colorful or passionate, but gray and listless—a sad parody of the passion you were born to glean from love.

---

*"There is a huge space between us,
and it keeps filling up with all the
things we do not say to each other."*
—From the film *Mr. & Mrs. Smith*

A relationship with good, honest fights would be preferable to familiar, convenient, and boring. Fighting mobilizes a life force that a boring relationship misses. When the flame of your spirit is reduced to an ember, you are in far more trouble than when that flame is raging. Boredom is as serious a wake-up call as constant upset. If you are bored, do something about it before you and your relationship dribble into oblivion.

CAN YOU HAVE A HAPPY ENDING?

In many on-again, off-again relationships, *any* ending would be happy. The very fact that both partners quit the game is a strong and healthy move. Yet there are several ways such a relationship could turn out, depending on what the partners are ready to choose:

1. *Ideal Scenario:* Both partners decide that they have had enough of the roller coaster and do the inner work to harmonize and stabilize. They may attend a relationship seminar or counseling together, and

both share a sincere desire to make the relationship work, followed with action that gets results.

2. *Effective Scenario:* Both partners decide that they have had enough of the roller coaster and that the relationship is not feeding them and probably will not. They consciously part as friends and move on to new and healthier relationships.

3. *Common Scenario:* One partner decides that he or she has had enough of the roller coaster and refuses to fuel the drama anymore. That person leaves the relationship, while the other partner, still invested in the drama, pursues the partner who left and attempts to keep him or her in the unhappy dance.

4. *Undesirable Scenario:* One or both partners decide to call it quits, but one or both become anxious about the relationship and for a long time harbor doubts and wonder if they should reunite, diminishing as well the quality of future relationships.

Very often when people leave a tumultuous on-again, off-again relationship, they are propelled into more stable situations. The roller-coaster ride built up both desire and momentum for change. If so, you may count the relationship as a service in the big picture of your relationship journey. Sometimes it takes a while and a bunch of experience under your belt to set you up for a successful partnership. And when you do create one, it is all the sweeter for its contrast

with all that preceded it. So you may count the experience as
your friend.

You are not a beggar at the banquet
of life. You are its honored guest.

—*Emmanuel (Pat Rodegast)*

WHAT YOU CAN DO ABOUT IT, POINT BY POINT

- Recognize the frustration or exasperation that an on-
  again, off-again relationship creates.
- Ask yourself what fears within you are running your
  part of the relationship, consider what you would do if
  you were not afraid, and do it.
- Speak your truth to your partner, and trust that your
  expression will ultimately lead to better.
- Refuse to be bored and get yourself unbored by mobi-
  lizing your passion.
- Use a relationship that hasn't been working as a motivator for the change you seek.

When Sex Gets Real

—∿—

Carla grew up in a religion that imposed strict judgments about sex. When she became a sexually active adult, Carla felt quite guilty. She was a passionate woman and loved her boyfriend. Yet when they had sex, she usually felt bad afterward. In fact, the more she enjoyed it, the worse she felt.

In our coaching session, Carla spoke about her intimate life with her boyfriend. "Sometimes in the afternoon we have an active nap," she explained.

"An active nap?" I asked, trying to understand.

A sly smile spread over Carla's face. "You know..."

"You mean sex?"

"Yes, that's it," she answered, blushing, "...you know."

I was amazed. Carla was an attractive thirty-four-year-old professional woman with wisdom and heart. Yet when it came to sex, she was still about ten years old emotionally.

Carla is an extreme example of many people who have blind

spots when it comes to sex. They want and enjoy sex, but have a hard time opening fully to a sexual partner. Or they go to the opposite extreme and use sex as a substitute for love rather than a bridge to it. Or they have difficulty communicating about it.

I explain to them that sexual fears or upsets are not problems, but opportunities to unlock doors to hidden rooms where great riches await. There they can claim the sacred marriage of passion and spirit.

Many people are fine with relationships until the issue of sex comes up. Or they dive into sex before they truly know their partner, and things get weird. Even if you think you know your partner, things may get weird. Yet weirdness—like wonderfulness—lives in your mind more than your genitals; so if you want to change your sex life, the place to do it is not between your legs, but between your ears. Someone said that sex is the thing that takes the shortest time that gets you into the longest trouble. But is that necessarily so? Can we let sex take a longer time and lead to the longest pleasure?

SEXUAL TICKETS TO DATING HELL

Your sex life is as unique as you are and cannot be prescribed or legislated by people other than you. Society, religion, parents, and peers have all kinds of ideas about sex, some of which may apply to you, and many of which may not. Since you are the one who has to live with yourself and your choices, you have to find confidence in the sex life of your own choosing. Who you have sex with, how often, and how is intensely personal. The question to hold your sexual experiences up to is: *Is the way I am having sex enhancing the quality of my life, or diminishing it?* If it is adding to your joy and life force, you are good to go. If not, take another look.

Top Ten Ways Your Sex Life Can Lead to Dating Hell:

1. You use dates as an excuse to get sex (generally a guy thing).
2. You use sex as an excuse to get dates (generally a woman thing).
3. You fall back on sex as a substitute for intimacy or facing uncomfortable relationship issues.
4. You use sex as a manipulation to get what you want (e.g., climbing the corporate or entertainment industry ladder).
5. You withhold sex as a manipulation to get what you want.
6. You let guilt keep you from enjoying sex.
7. You wait to have sex when you would rather do it.
8. You have sex when you would rather not.
9. You have promiscuous sex, anonymous sex, or affairs to escape from fears of intimacy.
10. You get pregnant, or get someone pregnant, without thinking about it beforehand or both partners agreeing.

SEXUAL TICKETS OUT OF DATING HELL

There are only three good reasons to have sex. Don't get prone without them:

1. Enjoyment
2. Connecting with your partner at a heart, soul, spiritual, or intimate level
3. Procreation

You may prioritize these reasons as you wish, or mix and match them, but in any order they are the keys to a great sex life. If, however, you find yourself stuck in one of the ten dating sex snares above, here are the tools that will get you free:

1. *Authenticity.* Being true to yourself counts for more than anyone else's ideas of what you should or should not do under the sheets. Lots of the rules people make up around sex are just plain screwy. Ayatollah Khomeini told his followers, "A man can have sex with animals such as sheep, cows, camels, and so on. However, he should kill the animal after he has his orgasm. He should not sell the meat to the people in his own village; however, selling the meat to the next door village should be fine." Ridiculous as this sounds, some of the things you have been told about sex, and have lived by, are not much saner. Living at peace with yourself is sane, and living at war with yourself is insane.

2. *Honest Communication.* The more up-front you are with your partner about what you feel and want, the better your sex life will be. Any form of deception, withholding, or manipulation will come back to

haunt you. If you want to create a sexual relationship or improve the one you already have, speak up about what you would like or not like. Open expression will get you and your partner more mileage than mind reading will.

3. *Connection.* Of course kissing and touching and sloshing around are tons of fun, but the most fun is feeling connected. Kindness, respect, and appreciation will take your sex life far beyond even the greatest physical sensations. Because we are spiritual beings at our core, it is the spirit in which we live that makes or breaks any experience. Sex is no exception. Spiritualize your sex by making love to the person inside the body. Embrace all of your partner, and you will enjoy many levels of orgasm simultaneously.

TIMING

How soon should you have sex with someone after beginning dating? I don't suggest diving into the sack immediately. Sometimes that works out, but often it doesn't, for the following reasons:

1. You don't really know who you are getting involved with. You are likely seeing more of your illusions about this person than who he really is. We are all very good at making up stories about people based on who we want them to be—very few of which are

true. Spending quality time with a person before unzipping puts you in a better position to make a wise decision about who you are partnering with. If he is wonderful, you will find out, and if he is creepy, you will find out. If your partner can't wait and is pressuring you, all the more reason to wait. Good connections can stand the test of not having immediate sex.

2. Sexual intimacy often brings up issues that require a platform of connection to deal with. Many women equate sex with romance, and if they sleep with someone, they assume an ongoing or committed relationship. Meanwhile, many men just wanna have fun and aren't much thinking about what's down the road. If one of you was sexually abused as a child or adult, deep feelings come forth when sexuality is stimulated. If you have a foundation of caring or communication, you stand a far better chance of dealing with your feelings and expectations than if you don't know each other.

Don't have sex, man. It leads to kissing and pretty soon you have to start talking to them.
—Steve Martin

So check in with yourself before checking into the hotel. Something inside you knows. You may get a green light, or red, or yellow. Watch for signs and take good care of youself.

GOOD VIBRATIONS

Sex for one? There may be times when the helping hand you seek is at the end of your own arm. Though many religions and authorities prohibit masturbation, lots of the people who made the rules against it were perfecting the skill. President Bill Clinton fired surgeon general Joycelyn Elders when she issued an educational statement that masturbation may be natural. (I'm sure the president's decision was political, not personal.) I know a woman who felt guilty about masturbating until she decided it was a great way to practice loving herself. She would take a hot bath, place candles and incense around her, put on her favorite music, and pleasure herself as she would have a lover do. Sometimes you are your own best lover.

Masturbation is not healthy when it becomes a substitute for having a sexual relationship with another person. If masturbation is your only sexual outlet to the exclusion of connecting with another human being, it may be time to face issues that, when understood, will bring you far more reward than isolating yourself. Ask yourself what it is you fear in being with a lover that you do not fear in being with yourself. If you can get past that resistance and allow someone into your heart and bed, you will double your pleasure.

RETURN TO INNOCENCE

While there are many excellent books on sexual techniques and power lovemaking (you can spot them easily on the shelves— they're the ones with the bent covers and frayed edges), I can safely give you the essence of what you need to know:

> *You already know how to be a great lover and give and receive immense joy and pleasure in lovemaking.*
> *Trust your instincts, do what flows naturally, and don't do what grates against you.*

Consider this account from John Perkins, an American who lived for many years with the Shuar, a primitive tribe in the remote jungles of Ecuador. John discovered that the Shuar had a healthy, playful, and in many ways enlightened attitude toward sex. Free of hang-ups or obsessions, the Shuar fine-tuned their sexual practices to an art and science. For example, the Shuar make love only in nature. They feel that being in the great outdoors increases their sense of oneness with the universe and with their partner. They practice a sophisticated *Kama Sutra*–like system in which the elders teach young adults the secrets of lovemaking in a gentle, respectful way. Over time, John found that his hosts had far happier sex lives than most of the people he knew back home.

One day several tribespeople asked John, "How do people in your culture learn about lovemaking?"

"Well," John answered hesitantly, "a couple of fifteen-year-old kids find their way to the backseat of a car, and they figure it out."

"My God," the Shuar elders exclaimed, aghast. "How primitive!"

So even though our society is on the cutting edge of technology, we may be in kindergarten sexually. We could use some tutoring from "primitive" people who are still in touch with the innocence we lost while developing our intellects at the expense of our hearts. Space, it turns out, may not be the final frontier. It may be the bedroom.

I could obviously write a great deal more about sex. Yet the simple truths here, applied wisely, can answer an entire realm of issues and deliver healing where more complicated strategies leave us wanting. Sex is the most natural experience in the world, but we have loaded it with judgments, fears, beliefs, and edicts that make us feel separate and alone rather than enlivened and connected. Your sex life is sacred and personal. When you find the confidence to live it as you choose, you come home to yourself.

WHAT YOU CAN DO ABOUT IT, POINT BY POINT

- Let your sex life be an expression of your true choices and desires, independent of what others have told you that you should be doing.
- Authenticity, communication, and focus on connection are your three most important tools to resolve sexual issues and move into celebratory sexual experiences.
- Get to know your partner before going to bed with her. Make sure you are making love with a person rather than with your fantasy about who she might be.
- Self-pleasuring can be a healthy or unhealthy sexual

expression, depending on whether it brings you greater connection with self or distances you from others.

- Behold your sex life through the eyes of innocence, and trust your natural instincts.

Is Make-Up Sex Worth the Fight?

〰️

Joey and Ashleigh had great chemistry in bed. Highly passionate, their sex life together outshone what they'd experienced with all previous lovers, and sometimes they spent whole weekends in the sack.

After a while Joey moved in with Ashleigh, and the two declared themselves an item. They were proud to be seen with each other, and their friends noticed the rosy glow on their cheeks.

Soon, however, the couple began to bicker, at first over little things, then over more fundamental issues. Joey tended to be possessive, and the more demanding he became, the more Ashleigh's hackles went up. Meanwhile, Joey was put off by Ashleigh's radical mood swings. Over time, their passion morphed to open hostility, and warfare became their dominant theme.

Then a pattern emerged: Just when the couple's issues would come to a head and they were about to strangle each other, one partner would initiate sex—the only arena in which they consistently connected well. For a moment Ashleigh and Joey would forget about their upsets and merge in sensual delight.

The heady feeling would last a few days, and the couple would be relaxed and affectionate. Then, like clockwork, their upsets would resurface and the fighting would begin again, escalating until days or weeks later when they found their way to the bedroom.

Certain animals, like the rhinoceros, have bizarre mating habits. The male and female will fight almost to the death, and if they survive, they will mate. Not far away in the jungle, the male praying mantis cannot copulate while its head is attached to its body; the female initiates sex by ripping the male's head off. If this reminds you of anyone you know, read on.

There is good news and bad news about the rhinoceros syndrome. The good news is that if you have a rocking sexual connection, you have a good thing going. The fire of a passion burns strong and nourishes you at a core level. God created juicy sex for a reason, and if you have found it, you are quite fortunate.

The bad news, if you are doing the rhino thing, is that you have settled for a life of warfare in exchange for a few moments of bliss. This formula has nothing to do with love and should not be confused with intimacy. If you need to fight to enjoy sex, you are wasting your time except for the sex.

There are many psychological reasons folks hurt each other for long periods as a prelude to getting it on: latent anger; bitterness toward the opposite sex; a sadomasochistic need to punish or be punished; belief that deep pleasure requires deep pain; replication of a parental pattern; addiction to drama, sex, or both; manipulation to keep a partner controlled; the adrenaline rush of nearly losing your partner and then reeling him in; and so on. We won't delve into the pathology here; I'll leave that to your friendly neighborhood shrink. Instead, let's turn our attention to how to undo it:

1. *Recognize the pattern.* Many couples keep acting out the script without noticing that it keeps replaying itself like a stuck CD. They think that's just the way relationships are. *Not so.* But if it's all you've ever seen or known, you may not recognize any other options.

2. *Notice the contrast* between how great you feel when you are emotionally connected with your partner and how distressed you feel when you are at odds. When you are upset, you get balled up energetically, your heart shuts down, and you feel separate, edgy, and off center. *Yuck.* When you are on the same wavelength as your lover, you are open, clear, and energetic, and your creative juices are flowing. You look kindly upon your partner and ponder ways to express your love for her. How much better does that feel?

3. *Create a preplanned signal to break the pattern in the midst of it.* As suggested earlier for people who over-analyze, agree during a peaceful moment what one or both of you will do when you recognize you have slipped into your fighting rut. If one of you makes the time-out sign, you each take twenty minutes

alone. Or you stop together, be silent, and each take five deep breaths. You will be amazed to see how powerfully you can stop a pattern in its tracks with a single moment of awareness.

4. *Find ways to enjoy passionate connection even when you're not in bed.* Do continue your great sex, but don't depend on it to feel good. Sex is just one domain among many in which lovers can pleasure each other. You can make love with thoughtful words; gentle caring touch; play; sharing mutual interests like music, dance, art, and film; fine dining; reading to each other; or a well-placed smile. There are millions of ways to create passionate chemistry without physical orgasm. The ancient art of tantric lovemaking teaches partners how to maintain an orgasmic relationship without depending on sexual release. You can turn your whole life into a love-making adventure that will not detract from your physical sex, but will instead enhance it.

5. *See a counselor, individually or together.* Facing your issues in the presence of a conscious professional can shift the energy that keeps you at odds, bring you closer to each other, and give you tools to upgrade. In a healthy forum you can learn to appreciate your lover not just as your sexual savior, but as a great learning partner.

DIRECT YOUR PASSION

If you are caught in the fight, fight, fight, fight . . . sex syndrome, you have a lot of electricity to work with, and you are in a far better position than couples who are dying of boredom. Use your energy to bring you closer together in more productive ways. When the mystic scientist Nikola Tesla laid eyes on Niagara Falls, he saw it not just as an overwhelming torrent, but as an infinite source of energy that could be channeled toward productive uses. Thus he developed alternating current electricity (AC), which powers our world today.

Likewise, you can take the energy you are investing in combat and reinvest it in feeling good more often. Consider the scientific fact that if you yelled for eight years, seven months, and six days, you would have produced enough sound energy to heat up one cup of coffee. As far as I'm concerned, a cup of coffee would not be worth that amount of trouble to go to. There are other ways to get a good cup without exhausting yourself for a long time. You could rechannel all that energy to do things that brought you reward, not warfare.

So it sits with a rhino-syndrome relationship. See the passion you find in the bedroom not as a release from warfare, but as a model of what you can feel with each other outside the bedroom and more of the time. Then your make-up sex will be transformed to wake-up sex, and you will have it all.

WHAT YOU CAN DO ABOUT IT, POINT BY POINT

- Recognize your pattern of fight, fight, fight, fight . . . sex.
- Evaluate the sharp contrast between cost and payoff.

- Consider the possibility that you can enjoy great sex without having to battle as a prerequisite.
- Agree on a signal to break the pattern in its midst, and put the signal into action.
- Find ways to rechannel your conflict energy into passionate activities outside the bedroom.

Let the One in Least Fear Lead

—∿∿—

Eddie and Thomas arrived at the hotel in St. Barts after a long and grueling flight. For months they had awaited their first vacation together, and they were both excited and anxious. Eddie had high hopes for their new relationship, and he wanted everything to be just right.

When they reached the reception desk, the clerk informed Eddie that the hotel had no record of their reservation. Eddie, generally short-tempered, grew upset and produced his notes on the reservation. The agent still could find no record, and an argument ensued. The interchange became more heated until it escalated into a shouting match.

Thomas, calmer than his partner, watched for a while and then interrupted, "Excuse me—regardless of what happened with the original reservation, do you have a room for us now?"

Eddie and the clerk stopped in their tracks, both looking a bit stunned. The clerk checked the computer for a few moments, and answered, "Well, yes, we do."

"Very well," Thomas replied. "We'll take it."

Five minutes later the couple was in their room. If it were not for Thomas's levelheaded intervention, the other two might still be arguing at the desk.

When facing an ambiguous or challenging situation as a couple, it is likely that one of you will be more peaceful and one of you will be more upset. At such a moment, the one who is calmer is in the best position to make a healthy decision. All upset stems from fear, so you may safely rely on the maxim, "Let the one in least fear lead."

Over time, you and your partner take turns being in greater and lesser fear than each other. In some situations you will be clearer, and in other situations your partner will. Once you sense who is more at peace at a given moment, one of you can say, "I'm feeling pretty riled about this, so perhaps you should make the call." Or, "You look pretty distraught; would you like me to do the speaking here?" If you can trust this principle and act on it, you will save yourself lots of trouble and create far more success.

A Course in Miracles, advising on relationships, suggests that you are safe as long as one of you remains sane at any given time. If your partner is upset and you remain grounded, you are safe. If you are anxious and your partner keeps his head on straight, you are safe. But if both of you lose your cool simultaneously, you are in a poor position to deal with each other or with anyone else. At such a time your best move is to stop, take a breather, and do what you can to regain sanity. Then, when at least one of you regains composure, you are in a good position to revisit the issue and make wise decisions.

THE PLIGHT OF PITY PARTNERS

The purpose of a relationship is to draw forth and reinforce each other's strengths. Some couples, however, use their relationship to reinforce each other's limits or sense of victimization and become "pity partners" by agreeing on what's wrong. In such a case you set up or perpetuate problems that you might have avoided if at least one of you stayed aligned with your strength.

Tony and Beth, for example, met at a health seminar. Both had had chronic illnesses and did not like doctors. They discovered they had a lot to talk about, especially their aches and pains and horror stories about their experiences with the medical profession. They were also stringent environmentalists, outraged by the atrocities committed against nature by unthinking people.

The couple began to date and eventually married. Most of their discussions centered on their ailing health, which never seemed to improve, and ecology, which seemed to be disintegrating the more they learned. Tony and Beth joined various protest organizations and made friends with like-minded people who agreed with their outrage. No matter what Tony and Beth did, they seemed to be limited by people and circumstances outside them, which only fueled their disdain.

Although Tony and Beth meant well and sincerely wanted to feel better and improve the environment, they did not realize that their constant focus on problems was keeping them stuck in the difficulties they were trying to remedy. Whatever you give your attention to expands, and whatever you agree on becomes (perceived) reality. Continually agreeing on what is wrong only makes things more wrong. Uniting against a common enemy does not strengthen you, but instead it ultimately weakens you. Attitude is the progenitor of conditions, so if you intend to change your life or the world, the place to begin is with your attitude.

The best way to help your partner is to not agree with their limits, which is equivalent to holding the vision of their possibilities. If he believes he is powerless against forces beyond his control and you concur, you hurt him more than you know. If she talks herself into hell and you go there with her, both of you will get fried. Stand on higher ground, however, and extend your partner a hand to step out, and you will both be free.

PIVOTING ON INSULTS

One common form of pity partnership is to agree on slights and hurts rendered to you by other individuals or couples. You may be insulted by mutual friends who say unkind things, do not return favors, abuse your trust, or do not include you in their activities. "Can you believe they didn't invite us to their party?" you huff. "That's so mean," your partner agrees; " . . . after all we did for them." Certainly friends or neighbors may say unkind words or do thoughtless acts—let's face it, stuff happens. Yet what they said or did, no matter their motivation, is less important than what you do with it. You can use an insult to practice your wholeness and freedom no matter what anyone else does, or you can let someone else rule your emotions. How you speak to your partner in the aftermath of a perceived slight is crucial. You can put him over the edge of self-destructive upset, or help him to simply not go there.

LET THE ONE IN LEAST FEAR LEAD

Herein lies your power to create a world that works for you or rips you off at every turn.

You may believe that your goal in relationships is to find a partner who will rally to your cause no matter how outraged you are, or that is the role you need to play for your partner. It is not so. The true purpose of a relationship is to help each other grow beyond fear. To throw gasoline onto a pyre of upset only fuels the flames. To take your partner to a cool pool where she can quench her spiritual thirst and regroup before acting hastily is a supreme gift. Taking a breath before speaking a harsh word can save you a world of trouble in its aftermath, and build character that will serve you for a lifetime.

ONE ACT OF CONFIDENCE CAN CHANGE A RELATIONSHIP AND A LIFE

When a young writer received the twelfth rejection of his manuscript, he threw it in the trash can. "That's it!" he exclaimed. "Either I'm just not fit to be a writer, or no one appreciates my work. I give up." Dismayed and discouraged, he threw himself into bed and fell off to sleep.

The young man's wife, observing his reaction, said nothing, but quietly removed the manuscript from the trash and set it neatly on his desk. In the morning when her husband sat at his desk, she placed her hands on his shoulders and told him, "I think you are a great writer and this manuscript is really good. Why don't you try sending it out one more time?"

The author agreed, and sent his book proposal to one more publisher. This time it was accepted and published. The title of the book was *The Power of Positive Thinking*, and the young writer was Dr. Norman Vincent Peale. The book went on to become a perennial classic, selling many millions of copies over half a century. Dr. Peale went on to be a force for positive change, uplifting the lives of countless millions. What a gift Mrs. Peale gave her husband and the world by believing in his possibilities rather than agreeing with his limits! In that moment the one in least fear led, and the world is a far better place for it.

You may not be interested in becoming a world-renowned author, but you do have a destiny of greatness in some domain. Simply being a good mother, for example, is a domain of intrinsic greatness. There is a niche for you in the scheme of success, and your relationship can be a valuable tool for you to arrive. When the one in least fear leads, you hasten that arrival and make the journey all the more enjoyable.

WHAT YOU CAN DO ABOUT IT, POINT BY POINT

- When you and your partner are confronted by a difficult situation, choice, or person, let the one of you who is in least fear lead.
- Do not form an alliance with your partner based on agreeing to limits or victimization. Instead, be sure that one of you sees and offers a higher road.
- Use insults or affronts not to reinforce your opposition to a common enemy, but to pivot and affirm your independence from the good opinion of others.
- Argue for your possibilities, not your problems.
- One small act of remembering greatness in the face of challenge can change a life, a relationship, and the world.

YOU TRY TOO HARD.

You can want a great relationship so badly that your efforts to create one stand in the way of its happening. More people sabotage romance by trying too hard than by not trying hard enough. There comes a point where relaxation, ease, and flow become stronger allies than continued effort. Knowing when to allow things to happen is equally as important as knowing when to make things happen. If you have been trying too hard, it's time to let go of your struggle and trust.

WHAT YOU CAN DO ABOUT IT

The following chapters will show you how to:

- Avoid pressuring your partner out of your relationship, or deal with anxious pressure from your partner.
- Let go of needing proofs of love, or deal with a partner who demands proofs of love.
- Disregard the illusions of "the perfect couple" and accept yourself and others as you are.
- Deal with the need to brag, or with a partner who brags.

Tell Me Today

—◆—

Marty and Harriet met at a singles party and began dating regularly. Harriet was anxious to get married, or at least have a committed relationship, and spent her time with Marty partly enjoying herself and partly sizing him up to see if he was going to make a commitment to her.

After a few months the couple took a vacation together to the Caribbean. There Harriet decided that she needed to know by the end of the vacation whether or not they were going to really be an item. She began to pressure Marty to make a decision. "Just tell me if we are going to have a relationship," she half-asked and half-demanded.

"We do have a relationship," answered Marty. "And it's a good one."

"I know," replied Harriet. "But I want to know if you are in it for the distance."

"I could be," Marty explained. "But we are still getting to

know each other. We've been seeing each other for just a couple of months, and this is the first time we've spent more than a day or weekend together. Let's just give it a chance."

"I don't want to waste my time if this is going nowhere," Harriet retorted, and stomped off in a huff, leaving Marty perplexed and frustrated.

I used to dine at a fine Italian restaurant that posted a notice at the bottom of their menu: *Please be patient. Good food takes time to prepare.* While I never liked waiting for the entrée, when it came I always enjoyed it more than fast food.

Trust would settle every problem now.
                                —A Course in Miracles

So it is with relationships. Even though Hollywood would like us to believe otherwise, good relationships rarely blip onto your screen out of nowhere and instantly you know you have met your soul mate and live happily ever after. The best relationships are those in which partners build their connection from the ground up, rather than depending on winning the relationship lottery.

If you deeply desire to meet your mate, the universe will do everything it can to send a great partner your way. But if you get antsy and uptight about achieving instant results, you will garble your receiver and jam the corridor through which your lover is trying to reach you. At such a point your best move is to chill out and trust.

> *Adopt the pace of nature: Her secret*
> *is patience.*
>
> *—Emerson*

The more pressure you exert to make a relationship happen, the more you push it away. No one likes to be forced to do what they don't want to do; even if they do want to do it, they want to do it by their own choice and timing. Trying to drag a commitment out of your partner, even if he or she may be ultimately willing, will only delay your progress.

TIME AND TIMING

The early Greek version of the Bible uses two different words for our word "time." One is *chronos*, referring to seconds, minutes, and hours. The other word is *kairos*, best translated as "when the time is ripe," or "in perfect timing," or "in God's time," signifying there is a right season and timing for everything.

Although we humans have our idea of when something is supposed to happen, life has its own idea. Sometimes life's timing matches our idea, and often it doesn't. Nature births things when it is ready, for its own good reasons. If you try to pluck a fruit before it is ripe, it is tasteless and may be poisonous. If you wait too long to harvest the fruit, it is putrid and nonnutritious. It takes patience and faith to flow with the natural order of readiness rather than try to force events according to your projections. Nature has great wisdom in timing, which will serve you if you let it.

Relationships have a timing, too. You may know you are right for each other instantly, or your connection may need time to reveal itself. Be less concerned with what is going to happen and more concerned with what is happening. If you are worrying about the future, you cannot see it clearly and your ability to make healthy choices is limited. If you live in the present, you open the door to the best possible results later. Is your time together fun, uplifting, and soul nourishing, or do you spend a lot of time struggling and arguing? Do you value your partner's company for who he is now, or are you waiting for something to happen before things will be okay? If it's not good now, it won't likely be good later. If you are enjoying each other now, you will likely enjoy each other more later. Trust your gut—it doesn't lie.

If Your Partner Is Pressuring You

- Deliver an honest, reasonable, and kind response, stating where you stand in your relationship and what you feel about being together.
- Do not get into a fight over the issue; that will make the issue more difficult for both of you to resolve.
- Look into your heart and find your truth about the relationship. If you want to develop it, say so. If you don't see that happening, say so. Your truth will be the greatest kindness to your partner and yourself.

WHEN NOT TO WAIT

Now for the other side of the coin: While you can smother a relationship if you try to force it before it is ready, it can wither on the vine if you hang in there too long. If your relationship has gone on for a long time and is going nowhere, put your cards on the table and ask your partner to do the same. When to speak up? Here are some clues:

- You are going in circles, having the same conversation over and over.
- Your partner still wants to see other people (or is), after being with you for a considerable time.
- Your partner can't seem to make up her mind if she wants to be with you.
- You are fighting more than loving.
- You feel more alone and frustrated than connected and fulfilled.

While you may not want to rock the boat, if the boat is sinking, some rocking might help. Consider your relationship as objectively as you can, and ask yourself where you are in the timing continuum. Is the fruit ripening, ripe, or past ripe? Can you relax and trust the process, or are you so frustrated and confused that you need to ask your partner to look at this issue with you? Remember, there is no rule that applies in all situations. Ask your inner knowing, and you will get your answer.

LET CONFIDENCE CALL THE SHOTS

By now you have likely noticed a theme that runs through all of our lessons:

When fear calls the shots, your love life sucks.
When self-trust, confidence, and inner knowing call the shots,
your love life rocks.

If you have to know right now, today, this minute, if your partner is going to be yours, fear is calling the shots. If you can breathe, trust the process, and tune in on what is appropriate for today, you will be shown answers that anxious forcing could never reveal.

Imagine, too, that life, God, the universe, or your inner wisdom wants you to know as much as you want to know. In fact, life is sending you all kinds of signals and guidance at every moment. Your job is to stay open to the messages. They will come and you will recognize them.

Relationship is more of a dance than a goal line. Every moment bears a gift. Find and accept the gift of this moment, and it will lead to many more.

WHAT YOU CAN DO ABOUT IT, POINT BY POINT

- If you are anxious about knowing if your partner is the one for you, relax before making any major decisions. Let confidence, not fear, call your shots.
- Stating your truth and asking from a place of love will yield you faster and better results than pressure.

- Enjoy the now moment as a stepping-stone to enjoying future moments.
- If someone is pressuring you, look inside yourself for your honest answer and speak it with kindness.
- Try to determine whether your relationship is still ripening, ripe, or overripe for a commitment.

Prove You Love Me

———— ᪥ ————

Brenda fell passionately in love with Josh and moved in with him. For a while everything was rosy, and the couple talked seriously about marriage.

Then Brenda grew more demanding. She expected very specific behaviors from Josh to prove he loved her: She wanted him to kiss her before he left for work; bring her flowers when he came home; drive the car when they traveled together; and numerous other items on her love-sign laundry list. When Josh did not remember or would not comply with all of Brenda's requests, she barraged him with complaints and criticisms that sent the couple into a tailspin.

In counseling with Brenda, she and I had this dialogue:

Alan: *Why are these particular acts so important to you?*

Brenda: *When Josh does them, I know he loves me.*

Alan: *So you just want to feel loved.*

Brenda: *That's right.*

Alan: *If you knew you were lovable, would you need Josh to prove he loves you?*

Brenda: *I guess not. If I knew I was lovable, I wouldn't need anyone to prove it.*

If you constantly set up tests to prove whether or not your partner loves you, you will both lose. You will lose because you have given your partner the power to validate your worth. Your partner will lose because he will have to keep dancing to live up to your requirements. It is not your partner's love you need. It is your own.

We all have desires that, when fulfilled, keep us happy and let us know we are attractive and valuable. Perhaps you like him to notice when you wear a new sexy dress or take you to dinner at your favorite restaurant. Or you feel bolstered when she gets excited over the car you have had your eye on or when she gives you a neck rub after a hard day at the office. In a good relationship partners are sensitive to their mate's desires, and they make an effort to support that person.

When tests of love grow into demands, you shoot your relationship in the foot. People who recognize their beauty and worth do not need others to constantly affirm it. If you find yourself demanding specific regular actions to confirm your partner's dedication, confront your own inner tyrant rather than projecting it onto your partner. Ask yourself, "What do I think I need from my partner that I cannot give myself?" If you can identify what you believe you are lacking and then give it to yourself, you will free both you and your partner, and get results that pressure could never yield.

What I believe I need from my partner: _____.

How I could give this to myself: _____.

EACH IN CHARGE OF YOUR OWN HAPPINESS

If your partner sets you up as the answer to her prayers or the source of her happiness and you agree to fill that role, you are both in for a wild and wacky ride. If you are responsible for your partner's fulfillment, you will also be responsible for her lack of fulfillment. Though it may be tempting to be your partner's dream girl or knight in shining armor, ultimately each of you will have to make your own selves happy. I know this doesn't sound very romantic, but it's just the way it is. You can still enjoy deep love and romance, but it will be even more powerful if you identify the source of that romance from inside yourself, not from your partner. To the extent that your partner can save you, she can crucify you. No one deserves that power, nor do they truly have it, unless you give it to them. Keep the power of your happiness where it was given—in your own hands—and you will both sit at the helm of your own well-being.

It takes only a six-inch fall for a halo
to become a noose.

—Source unknown

HOW TO DEAL WITH A DEMANDING PARTNER

If your partner asks a lot of you to prove your love, find a balance between giving him what he wants and helping him to recognize his wholeness no matter what you give him. Say, for example:

> *(Name), you know I love you very much and I want you to be happy. I want to do everything I can to support you to feel good and give you the things you want. There also may be times when I cannot offer you what you are asking for. Sometimes I may forget, or I may not be open or willing to give at the moment. This does not mean that I care about you less. Please try to understand in those moments, and I assure you there will be lots of times when I can do for you things that please you.*

This will hopefully ease your partner's upset. Like Brenda above, your partner just wants to know that he is loved. If he feels that from you, the particular acts won't be a big issue.

If your partner remains upset, it may be time for you to step back and allow him to work it out for himself. I don't recommend long processing sessions around the issue. It may be time for your partner to get some coaching or counseling to find the place inside himself that is whole and not dependent on you to stay happy.

LOVE NEVER TESTS

Only people insecure need to test love. Rather than setting your partner up to prove her dedication, prove your dedication to yourself by letting her off the hook. Consider what you can give to your partner rather than what you can get from her. Relationship acts that proceed from fear usually backfire, and those that proceed from generosity of spirit bear far-reaching results.

If you are ever tempted to set up a particular act as a test or symbol of your partner's love, ask yourself, "How would a confident, self-assured person deal with this?" Then try to find a place of self-assuredness inside you. If you can—and you can—you will be amazed at the different perspective you gain and the results that follow.

Draw forth your ideal lover by appreciating and celebrating the acts of love he does, and waste no time complaining about what he doesn't do. If you look just a bit deeper, you may find that your ideal lover may already live inside your present one.

WHAT YOU CAN DO ABOUT IT, POINT BY POINT

- Avoid setting up particular acts as proof of whether or not your partner loves and cares about you.
- Communicate to your partner what is important to you, but do not demand it.

- Identify what you think you need from your partner, and then see how you can give it to yourself.
- If your partner is demanding, inform her that you love and care about her, and do what you can to give her what she asks for. Do not, however, let demands dictate a relationship.
- If you are tempted to test your partner, ask yourself what a self-assured person would do in this situation, and try to tap in to the place of confidence within you.

The Problem
with Perfect Couples

—∿—

Keith and Amy had it all going for them. Both of them attractive, charismatic, successful, and obviously very much in love, they were the envy of all of their friends. Keith would regularly extol his affection for Amy at public gatherings, and the couple even appeared on a local television show with a psychologist who used them as a model of a healthy relationship.

You can imagine the shock waves that went through the neighborhood when Keith was caught having an affair with a dance instructor. Amy was devastated, and all of their friends shook their heads in amazement.

The couple went through counseling, which unearthed issues the two had never faced. Keith admitted that this affair was not his first. Amy realized that she had gotten so caught up in maintaining a public image for herself and her marriage that she had drifted considerably from her valued connection with her husband and their daughter.

When I was last in touch with Keith and Amy, they were
doing their best to rebuild their marriage and their relationships with friends. This time they were more devoted to being
themselves than to being who they thought they should be and
whom others wanted them to be.

We all look to certain couples as role models of love, commitment, and a solid relationship. Yet in spite of appearances,
some relationships that look strong on the outside are shaky
on the inside. If they break up, we are shocked. "Carl and Sally
were the last couple I ever thought would get divorced!" you
exclaim. "I had no idea they were having problems." Then you
may begin to feel anxious or insecure about your own relationship or marriage: "If the Jamisons could fall apart, it could
happen to us." Yet such a shakeup is healthy if it moves you to
examine where you stand in your relationship, and to do what
it takes to stay perched on your cutting edge of aliveness.

Secure couples do not need to put on a show to prove their
connection. They teach more by example than by words.
Unhappy couples who try to convince you how blissful they
are are trying to convince themselves or offset their distress by
projecting an image to the contrary. Real happiness is its own
best testimonial and requires neither words nor a PR cam-
paign to sell it.

Some psychologists did a study of people who ooze long,
gooey public displays of affection when saying good-bye at airport gates. The experimenters found a direct relationship
between the ostentatiousness of their farewell and their insecurity in their relationship. The less secure the couple felt
("Maybe we won't see each other again," or, "I hope he doesn't

cheat on me when we're apart"), the longer and schmaltzier was their good-bye. Couples who were more established in their relationship were satisfied with a hug, kiss, and "Have a great trip, honey." Secure couples recognize the strength of their union and do not need to flash it on a billboard to each other or to the world. Insecurity, by contrast, calls for copious expression and continuous validation.

I am leery of individuals or couples who go out of their way to make profuse public expressions of their love. Usually, I have found, they are attempting to offset a private deficiency. A business associate of mine, Lars, invited me to an open-mike night at a local espresso café, where he read a gutsy original love poem to his fiancée. The engagement ended when Lars's fiancée received several phone calls from women Lars had been dating on his business trips.

The bigger the front,
the bigger the back.

—*Zen*

The point here is not that men cheat; many women also have an investment in presentation that is not backed up by reality. The point is that you cannot judge a couple by their appearance, and envy is never appropriate. The best couples do not make a spectacle of their romance, but burn a passionate love quietly, and their harmony is spoken by the light in their eyes rather than through public poems. You can never know or judge what is happening inside the heart of another; your job is to look within to see where you stand on the path prescribed by your own values.

DON'T PUT A NAME OR FACE ON IT

When seeking a quality partner or relationship, be less involved with how the relationship looks, and more involved with how the relationship feels.

The story is told of a man who walked into a restaurant with an ostrich and the two sat down for dinner. At the end of their meal the waitress delivered a check for $35.95. The fellow reached into his pocket, emptied all his bills and change, and came up with exactly $35.95 plus a 15 percent tip.

The following week the man and the ostrich returned, and the same waitress served them. This time the check totaled $47.11. He emptied his pockets and miraculously took out exactly $47.11 plus a 15 percent tip.

A week later the man and ostrich dined again with the same server. When the tab arrived, again he found the precise amount in his pockets.

By now the waitress was quite curious. She told the man, "I am astounded that you take this ostrich to dinner here every week and you always have the exact amount of money to pay your tab. How do you do that?"

"It's an amazing story," the fellow explained. "Several years ago while I was cleaning my basement I found an old bottle. When I opened it, a genie emerged and told me I could have two wishes. My first wish was to always have enough money to buy anything I want. Now, wherever I go, I simply reach into my pocket and the exact amount of money is there. You have seen me buy my meals this way. I have also purchased a car, house, and vacations. No matter how much anything costs, I find the precise amount in my pocket or checkbook."

"That's astonishing!" replied the waitress. "And what was your second wish?"

"To marry a chick with long legs."

This story is significant because it illustrates the difference between calling for a *particular trait* and calling for a *quality of experience*. When the man wished for a chick with long legs, he got it. His ultimate result wasn't what he really wanted, but the universe took him at his word and delivered it. When he wished for an ongoing experience of prosperity, he got that, too. So he was better off asking for an experience than an object. You always receive what you ask for, so think twice before asking.

Rather than trying to force a particular person to be your mate, ask for a kind of person or a quality of relationship. You can get the handsome, wealthy guy, but if he's an egotist, liar, or alcoholic, you end up losing. You also have the power to set your sights on a thoughtful fellow who stimulates your passion and enhances the quality of your life, and get that. (Who knows, you might end up with someone handsome and wealthy in the process.) One thing is for sure: when you set your intention for how you want to feel rather than how it looks, you will create far more satisfying results than asking for a shell with questionable contents.

PERFECT COUPLES

Perfect couples are perfectly human. They wake up with morning breath, occasionally drip mustard on their sweaters, have neurotic moments, and fight. Couples who are beautiful and happy all the time exist only in 1950s sitcoms and Disney movies (also see the film *Pleasantville*).

Save yourself time and torment by revisiting your idea of a perfect couple. A perfect couple is not propped up like figures on a wedding cake. They are real people with ecstasy and sadness, good days and off days, passions and reservations, in the process of discovering themselves and each other. They have not reached some tinsel-coated goal, but they are immersed in ongoing evolution. Some days they thank God for being together, and other days they wonder what they are doing together. They are a lot more like you than you know.

While disillusionment about relationships is initially painful, it is ultimately liberating. The only thing more devastating than disillusionment is to go on living in an illusion. You have heard that the truth hurts, but the only thing it hurts is fantasies. When you realize the gifts that a relationship with a real person offers you, illusions don't quite cut it anymore.

When your perfect neighbors' relationship begins to fall apart, despair not. Their process is as perfect for them as yours is for you. Take peace in the perfection of the big picture rather than what the newspaper society page proclaims. There is another couple just down the street who are still together and enjoying each other immensely. They have nothing to flaunt, but nothing to hide.

WHAT YOU CAN DO ABOUT IT, POINT BY POINT

- Do not envy perfect couples or put them on a pedestal; instead, respect them for their strengths and allow for weaknesses you may not see.
- Do not seek to present your relationship as perfect, for your perfection lies in ongoing evolution and growth.
- Do not put a name or face on your ideal partner. Instead, identify valued attributes and qualities of experience.
- Appreciate disillusionment as a doorway to hidden truth.

A Legend in His Own Mind

—∿—

Fred spent a great deal of time bragging about his sexual conquests. When he got together with his buddies, he spared them no details of the previous night's date. What Fred did not realize, in his efforts to show that he was *the man*, was that his friends were not impressed by his bravado. They listened politely, but made fun of him behind his back.

Fred's braggadocio spilled into his dating life as well. Ultimately he made an impact on women—but not the impact he wanted. Most women were repelled by Fred's need to crow about his exploits. As a result, Fred's relationships were brief and shallow; the longer his stories grew, the shorter his relationships became.

When Fred met Christine, she was the first person to be honest with him. "I like you, Fred, and I think you have some great qualities," she told him. "But I really don't need to hear about all the women you've bedded. You may be trying to impress me, but actually it turns me off. Do you think we could be together without dragging your past girlfriends into our conversations? That would be far more impressive to me."

Braggarts are insecure. They do not believe in themselves, their attractiveness, or their sexual prowess, so they try to compensate by pumping up the volume in public. Although they seek to impress friends and dates, they are really trying to impress themselves. In psychological terms, they are engaged in *reaction formation*—attempting to offset a perceived deficit by overblowing the presentation of its opposite.

> *He who knows, does not say. He*
> *who says, does not.*
> —*Lao Tse*

People who are confident in themselves and their abilities do not need to broadcast it. To the contrary, they may say nothing or play their accomplishments down. People who have great sex lives do not air them; they just enjoy them. It's the quiet ones you have to watch out for.

HOW MUCH DO YOU NEED TO CROW?

If you tend to boast about your exploits, consider why you want to, and the perceived rewards you receive. Do you recognize that you are enough without falling back on mentioning who you have bedded, who has pursued you, what celebrities you know, or how long your Hummer is? If you need such accolades to prove yourself, you are in deep doo-doo indeed.

The louder he spoke of his honor, the faster we counted the spoons.
—*Emerson*

There is so much more to you! You are worthy for who you are, not what you do; attractive for your essence, not your accomplishments. When you appreciate yourself for your character more than your conquests, others will respect you more and your relationships will be built on reality, not presentation. You will have real friends who will thank you to your face, not mock you behind your back. And you will attract quality dates, because they have found their way to your heart, rather than bought a ticket to your show.

HOW TO DEAL WITH A BRAGGART

Dating a boaster can be annoying, frustrating, and short-lived. If, however, you feel your partner has possibilities beyond his or her overblown presentation and you want to pursue the relationship, try the following:

1. Withdraw your attention (and your presence) when they go into their rap. Do not ask them questions, make comments, or reinforce them for their sounding off. Change the subject or step away.

2. Explain, like Christine above, that you like them for who they are and that you would like to develop your relationship based on what is happening between the two of you now rather than what they have already done. Reinforce them for authenticity rather than presentation.

3. Be even more direct: "I really don't want to hear any more about your former girlfriends. If you want to keep going out with me, you'll have to leave them behind."

Some braggarts will get the gist of your communication, and others will not. If your date looks at you with a dull stare, argues, or puffs his or her feathers even more, it's time to move on. Remember that every case is unique, and no book or belief system can prescribe what to do every time in a particular situation. Some partners will be motivated to show up more as themselves, and others will either intensify their braggadocio or leave. Even more important, you must choose what you are willing to accept and what you are not. Dealing with a braggart may be a powerful exercise for you to recognize what you value in a relationship and ask for it. Once you are clear, the way will be clearer.

WHAT YOU CAN DO ABOUT IT, POINT BY POINT

- Consider if you may brag to impress—stories of sexual conquest, accolades received, famous friends, expensive possessions, and anything else that may be perceived as ostentatious.
- Ask yourself what deficits you believe you have that

your boasting is intended to offset. Seek to find authentic, admirable, attractive qualities that make you worthy without showing off.

- If you are dating a braggart, withdraw attention from boastful tales and directly communicate your desire to be with a real person rather than a broadcaster of tall tales.
- Reward your partner for realness and humility if and when it shows up.

REASON #8.

COMMITMENT TERRIFIES YOU.

Commitment can be a scary thing. Unwise commitment can mess up your life, whereas well-chosen commitment can empower you immensely. It can also be difficult to deal with a partner who fears to commit. When is commitment necessary, and when is it okay to just flow with what is happening? Coming to peace with commitment, within yourself and your partner, can extricate you from painful arguments and help you both get what you want.

WHAT YOU CAN DO ABOUT IT

The following chapters will show you how to:
- Recognize how you may be avoiding commitment without knowing it.
- Come to peace with yourself whether you choose to commit, or not.
- Deal with a partner who fears or resists commitment.
- Know when to take a leap of faith and when to play it safe.
- Find the courage and confidence to take a leap when you are ready.

You Can't Hit a Moving Target

—◆—

Sheila was a flight attendant who had dates in every city where she landed. Attractive, upbeat, witty, and playful, Sheila had her pick of men. But she never dated anyone more than a few times.

In counseling, Sheila admitted that she really wanted a relationship, but she feared intimacy and commitment. At a young age she had been married for a few years, and the experience was a disaster. There was no way she wanted to repeat that painful episode.

When I asked Sheila how she had kept herself from falling in love or developing a lasting relationship with any of her suitors, her answer was telling: "It's simple: You can't hit a moving target."

You don't need to be a flight attendant gallivanting around the world to be an elusive target. You just need to keep moving so fast that no one can catch you.

People who are too busy to have a relationship are too busy by choice. If a relationship were important to them, they would slow down long enough to be available. But because such people equate intimacy with weakness, they guard their heart and stay one step beyond love's reach. If those who are overly busy took the time to stop and confront the monster at their heels, they would encounter a paper dragon. Then they would admit their true desire for connection, drop their defenses, and welcome love.

Social sprinters will tell you they are too busy to deal with their feelings—but *the very purpose* of their being so busy is to avoid having to face those feelings. My client Corinne was raised in a strict guilt-laden family; she graduated with honors from Our Lady of Perpetual Blame. Now Corinne feels so guilty about everything that she is terrified to be alone with herself; in the quiet she would have to face her overwhelming self-judgments. So Corinne generates an endless series of errands, projects, dramas, and emergencies to keep her constantly on the go. If she slowed down long enough to take a look at herself, she would not behold the ugly, evil woman she fears, but a beautiful radiant spirit. She would recognize her innocence and drop her needless running. People who feel fulfilled do not find distractions preferable to their own company or that of loved ones. Their relationships are enough because *they* are enough.

If you are running from love, consider what you are giving up for what you are getting: Connection for disconnection. Relaxation for rushing. Intimacy for isolation. Self-acceptance for guilt. Peace for drama. While part of you perceives safety in scurrying, it is not there. The only true sanctuary is the temple of your own heart. Find your home there, and darting about will lose its grip and appeal.

Dating lots of people in different places can be fun and

exciting. Enjoy, learn, and grow from the experience. Every encounter and relationship serves a purpose. At some point, though, ask yourself if you would like a deeper connection. Don't end up like the man who dug many shallow wells but died of thirst because he never dug deep enough in any one of them. If you dig deep enough in the right spot, you can tap in to a spring that will nourish you for a lifetime.

I'M AVAILABLE IF YOU'RE NOT

My friend Cliff revealed to me his personal variation on the theme of "catch me if you can—but you can't." Although Cliff dated many women, none of his relationships lasted more than a few months. He would tell his friends, "The women I want don't want me, and the women who want me, I don't want."

One day Cliff realized that he had unknowingly been playing out a script that dominated his relationships and kept him from being with someone he really liked: *a partner is acceptable to me as long as one of us is not available.*

If you keep attracting unavailable people, *you* are not available. Resist, deny, find excuses, or blame your loneliness on shoddy partners or cruel twists, but this is how it sits. Available people attract available people. Unavailable people either attract unavailable people or make themselves unavailable. You have far more of a say in who shows up, for how long, and why and how it ends than you have been taught or may admit. While you may be adept at throwing smoke screens up when someone gets too close, you can with equal deftness take those barriers down.

HOT PURSUIT OF A COLD POTATO

If you are dating a moving target, think about whether or not your connection is fulfilling you. Are you in love, or in the hope of love? Perhaps you and your partner both run in the fast lane, and your sex life resembles jets refueling in midair. If you enjoy this, carry on. The two of you are well matched, and you have your own version of a working relationship.

If, however, your partner lives on roller skates but you would like to slow down and grow a partnership, don't spend a lot of time chasing or waiting. Tell him you would like more time together, and ask if he is willing to cool his jets to explore that. If your speedy friend is not ready, he will find a million excuses. He may sincerely believe he has to spread himself thin—you know, work, and all that—but that does not match your vision. If you want a real person to be with, you are going to have to claim it—not so much with words, but with your intentions and actions. When you are sure of what you want and deserve, you will have it. Until then you will attract part-ners who mirror what you will settle for.

Just put forth a clear enough request,
and everything your heart desires
must come to you.
—Shakti Gawain

It is a rare speed freak who will slow down upon request. People in self-protection perceive safety in their defenses

unless they recognize a more attractive option. So your best
tack is not to pressure, argue, or give your partner an ulti-
matum. Your best tack is to be so clear in your value and desire
for presence that your partner is moved to meet you there. If
he can, he will. If not, don't belabor it. You have a life to live.

SPEED OR ESSENCE?

The world is moving faster every day. In many domains quality
and integrity have been compromised for speed. If you are
building microchips, processing speed is essential. If you are
building a relationship, presence and attentiveness to the relationship are essential. If you can be productive in your work
life and stay connected in your love life, you have achieved a
rare and crucial balance. This book offers you many tools to
help you do just that.

You have something to say about the speed at which you
move through your life. Whether you are untouchable or
touchable is entirely up to you. When you are ready to be
touched, you may trade in your roller skates for warm, loving
arms. It's not a bad deal, when you think about it.

WHAT YOU CAN DO ABOUT IT, POINT BY POINT

- If you are too busy for a relationship, evaluate both
  your payoff and your cost.
- Ask yourself what you fear would happen if you
  slowed down.
- If you keep meeting people who are not available,
  consider if you are available.

- If you are dating someone who is a moving target, ask yourself if this relationship is working for you. If not, invite your partner to be more present with you.
- Spend a day, weekend, or week with your partner without cell phones, e-mail, work, or any distractions from being fully present with each other.

Everything You Always Wanted to Know About Commitment-phobes (But Couldn't Get Them to Answer)

━━━∾∾∾━━━

An artist friend of mine had a poster on his wall that a girlfriend had given him: *"I would blow your mind if I could find it."* Grayson had a hard time committing to anything. Consequently, his friends could get only so close to him; he drove others crazy; and women would eventually throw their hands up and scurry away, befuddled.

Grayson had just gotten out of a marriage and was not about to be corralled again soon—which rendered his heart untouchable. He wanted love, but also feared it. So he weaved tangled push-pull, on-again, off-again relationships that gave him and his partners tastes of happiness, but ultimately left both him and his partners frustrated.

Dating someone who can't make a commitment is like trying to hug a greased watermelon. It's exasperating. Commitment-phobes are driven by three fears:

1. Making a wrong decision they will have to live with.
2. Entrapment, loss of freedom and independence.
3. Missing out on a better option.

HOW TO DEAL WITH A COMMITMENT-PHOBE

If you are with someone who has a hard time committing, not just to your relationship, but to almost anything, you have several options:

1. *Tell her directly* that you have a hard time dealing with her unwillingness to choose. Let her know that if she revealed her honest choices, you would have something to work with, you would both have more fun, and your shared ventures would be more effective.

2. *Be specific* about the things you need an answer on. Tell him you need a yes or no on this subject, and let him know when you need it. If he gives you no answer, just go ahead and do what you would like to do independent of his decision.

3. *Make strong decisions for yourself.* As you level the playing field with your clear choices, your partner will either step up to the plate or head for the showers.

4. *Is the issue on which you need a commitment crucial?* If not, it may not be worth hassling over. If it is, say so and explain why.

5. Give up trying to change your partner, and just *love and enjoy her for who she is.* Perhaps she is already perfect in her own unique way.

IF COMMITMENT SCARES YOU

If you have a hard time giving firm responses in relationships, consider these tips:

1. *You don't have to choose or commit.* You are free to never commit to anyone or anything if you don't wish to. Simply knowing this will release some of the pressure you feel that makes it difficult to see clearly or choose wisely. Now that you don't have to do anything, what would you like to do?

2. *Take an honest look at the fear that may be standing in the way of your choosing.* Have you been wounded or betrayed and are determined not to be hurt again? Have you observed uninspiring (or downright terrifying) role models of people who committed and lost? Do you fear losing control? Are you using your unwillingness to decide as a tool to hold power over your partner? The more clearly you can shine light on your issues, the more rapidly you will move beyond them. Discuss your fears candidly with a friend, coach, or counselor, and you will likely create movement.

3. Realize that *to choose is to empower.* Every time you make a clear choice, you grow in strength, effectiveness, and

peace. This is why it is important to make decisions firmly and avoid putting them off. The more decisions you put off, and the longer you put them off, the more stressed and confused you feel. Then, when you finally make the decision, you feel lighter, freer, and stronger, and you realize you could have done this a long time ago.

4. Remember that *often any decision is better than no decision*. In many cases you can make any choice work as long as you are fully behind it. There are many routes to the mountaintop. If you are true to yours, you will arrive more quickly and easily than if you sit around wondering.

5. Recognize that *you help your partner by making a decision*. If you drive people crazy with your indecisiveness, you will make their lives a lot easier if you give them something to work with.

Commitment is scary only if you regard it as an enemy that will disempower you. Reframe it as your friend, and it will serve you many times each day. Then you cease to resist commitment as the end of life, and embrace it as the beginning of a better one.

WHAT YOU CAN DO ABOUT IT, POINT BY POINT

If you are with someone who avoids commitment:
- Be specific about the issues for which you need an answer.

- Make strong decisions for yourself and set a tone of clear choice-making in the relationship.
- Seek to appreciate and enjoy your partner for who they are.

If you have difficulty with commitment:
- Be honest about the fears that stand between you and strong choices.
- Practice making choices, even on small things, to enhance your self-empowerment.
- See making clear choices as a way to serve and help your partner.

Look Before You Leap—
But Then Leap

———

At age fifteen I attended a summer camp where I developed a major crush on a cute girl named Roberta. Since the boys' and girls' sides of the camp were separate and the two groups rarely interacted, I saw Roberta only occasionally and at a distance. But when I did, my heart sang.

One evening the camp leaders took pity on our pining adolescent hormones and organized a coed excursion to a roller-skating rink. There I got up the nerve to invite Roberta to skate with me. We held hands for a few minutes, and I was in heaven. I didn't wash that hand for weeks. (Not that I washed it much anyway.)

I saw Roberta a few more times during the summer, but felt shy and tongue-tied when we were together. She was such a babe and I was such a dweeb, I figured. We said hi politely, but that was it.

Summer ended and we went home to separate cities. I thought often of Roberta, cherishing the evening I touched her and the few thrilling moments we connected. I dearly wished to meet someone else I felt so excited about.

Three years later I saw Roberta at a party. She was still so beautiful to me, and I felt that sparkle again. To my dismay, she showed me an engagement ring on her finger.

More confident at eighteen than at fifteen, I revealed my feelings for her. "When we were in summer camp, I had a huge crush on you," I confessed. "The night we skated together was the highlight of my summer. I have thought about you a lot since then."

A bittersweet smile grew on Roberta's face. "I have a confession, too," she admitted. "I had a crush on you. I remember that night very well."

You can imagine how shocked I was to hear this!

Then Roberta made a poignant comment that has affected thousands of my decisions to this day: "Who knows?" she mused. "If either of us had the guts to speak up then, this might have been your ring on my finger now."

It is said that when we come to the end of our life, it is not the things we did that we regret; it is the things we didn't do. Buddha taught, "There are two reasons great ideas never come to fruition: (1) not finishing, and (2) not beginning." So it goes for great relationships.

While many people err by diving into relationships too soon, others err by waiting too long to dive—or never diving at all. Such people stand shivering on the shore, feeling too shy or fearful to jump. They do not recognize that the aliveness they would gain by asking for what they want far exceeds the safety they perceive in hiding or waiting. Nor do they know their power and deservingness to enjoy what makes their heart sing. When you leap, often you will get what you want, and sometimes you will not—but in either case you will be ahead of where you were if you just sat wondering.

When I asked a seminar audience, "What would you do if you were not afraid?" A woman raised her hand and declared, "I would ask a certain man to go to a party with me this weekend." Feeling bold, I offered the woman my cell phone and asked her if she would be willing to phone him on the spot. Being a good sport, she agreed and stepped outside to make the call. Ten minutes later she returned with an enormous smile. "I have a date!" she proclaimed to the tune of wild applause.

When I returned to the same city a year later, I asked a friend of the woman if she had seen her recently. "I certainly have," her friend reported. "I went to her wedding on New Year's Day . . . She married the fellow she phoned at your seminar."

You may be closer than you know to having the relationship your heart desires. You might be but one phone call away. Though you may believe that your mate is far down the road, your key step may be a leap of faith. You may not need to lose ten pounds; get over your childhood sexual abuse trauma; come to terms with your ex; get financially stable; get rid of your current lover; move to Sedona; or . . . or . . . or . . . . God has not prescribed such prerequisites—*you* have. Just as you have made them up, you can step beyond them. Fear has many reasons not to love; love has one reason not to fear: It alone is real.

CAN YOU *NOT* DO IT?

If you are attracted to someone and you are not sure if you should pursue being with him, *don't*. Let go of the idea of getting together, and watch what happens. If you forget about him, your attraction was fleeting and without substance. But if you cannot get him off your mind; or you keep running into him; or he sends you signals that he is interested, you have your instructions.

Exercise:
Building your Leap Muscles

Fill in the blanks below, using any subject matter, not just relationships.

If I were not afraid, I would_____.
Someone I would like to have a date with: _____.
Someone I feel sexually attracted to: _____.
Someone I think would make a good relationship partner:_____.
Something I keep thinking about purchasing:_____.
A place I keep thinking about visiting:_____.
A creative pursuit I keep fantasizing about (writing, music, art, etc.:)____
_____.
What I would do if money were no object: _____.
What I would quit doing if money were no object:_____.
What I would do if I did not feel guilty:_____.
What I would quit doing if I did not feel guilty quitting:_____.
Someone whose lifestyle I would like to emulate:_____.
What I would speak up about if I were not shy or hesitant:_____.
My secret fantasy:_____.
Anything else that would be a leap for me:_____.

Recording your answers will move you toward making your visions a reality. I am not suggesting you do everything you have written, and I am not suggesting you not do it. Simply thinking about these ideas, identifying them, and experiencing the positive feelings they engender is a key step to making them happen. If you like, choose one item from your above responses that is most enlivening to you, and take a step in that direction.

WHEN NOT TO LEAP

There are two situations in which I would not recommend leaping:

1. *If your fear is far greater than your motivation*, you are at crosscurrents with yourself and you may sabotage your efforts. The way to overcome fear is not to buck through it, but to amp up your motivation and intention so that you tap in to momentum that is greater than the obstacle posed by the fear. Why do you want to do this? How could your life be better? What would be the best thing that could happen if you did this? When your excitement and enthusiasm exceed your resistance, fear loses its stopping power, and you will walk beyond it.

2. *If there is a good reason not to go ahead*, respect it. Here you must discern between "reasons" put forth by the voice of fear or smallness, and practical reasons suggested by wisdom. It may be a leap of faith to invest your life savings in that new stock your buddy is raving about, but you may be wiser to invest what you comfortably can and see how that does. Or it may be better to have a date with the woman across

the hall before purchasing the tickets for your Caribbean cruise together. Leaps of faith often fly in the face of reason, but also know when to respect it.

WHAT YOU SEEK IS SEEKING YOU

I saw a clever billboard ad for a classy sports car. The ad posted a photo of the auto, with the bold headline **"It wants you, too."** If you are seeking to sell a car or home, someone is searching for one just like the one you have listed. If you have particular career skills, a company needs exactly what you have to offer. If you have a vision of an ideal relationship partner, someone who matches your description is yearning to be with someone like you. Trusting this law of balance will empower you to seek and find what you want. Do not be quick to write off your desires as simply selfish; you will bring joy to someone as much as they will bring happiness to you.

Precautions, alertness, and due diligence are important. But so are adventure, stretching, and guts. Look before you leap. But when you have looked long enough, it's time to jump. You may be surprised to discover that what appeared to be an untraversable chasm was no wider than one courageous step.

WHAT YOU CAN DO ABOUT IT, POINT BY POINT

- Consider if the time for thinking about a step or preparing for it is over and it is time to move ahead.
- If someone or something keeps showing up in your mind or life, it may be a sign to act on it. Ask yourself, "Can I *not* do it?"

- After completing the "Building Your Leap Muscles" inventory above, consider which items speak to you most directly, and move on them.
- Do not leap if your fear is greater than your inspiration, or if there is a solid reason not to.
- Know that what you seek is seeking you.

YOU MISS THE OFF-RAMP ON THE ROAD TO THE ALTAR OF DOOM.

Marriage is a huge decision, perhaps the biggest of your life. Many people get married for the wrong reasons or choose partners unwisely, and regret it. Others choose from deep inner knowing and reap huge benefits. If you are aware of what makes a prospective marriage work and what doesn't, and how to choose a partner wisely, your marriage will be a blessing to you and your partner, and your relationship will bring you immense fulfillment.

WHAT YOU CAN DO ABOUT IT

The following chapters will show you how to:
- Recognize red flags if you are thinking about getting married.
- Avoid costly mistakes when choosing a partner.
- Know who to marry when you are ready.

Ten Questions to Ask Yourself
Before You Say, "I Do"

———

Anne: I was a total "Bridezilla"—so obsessed with my wedding that I lost sight of the relationship. Jim and I started our marriage forty thousand dollars in debt from the wedding. When we came home from the honeymoon, I got totally depressed. My whole life had led up to my wedding day, and now it was over. I had no purpose and no identity. It was then that my real relationship with Jim started.

Cindy: When Joe proposed to me, I was flattered. Happy, but not excited. When I told my best friend about the engagement, she reflected to me: "I can't really say I'm bowled over by your enthusiasm." That was the most helpful response anyone could have given me. I called off the engagement when I understood that marriage is such an important decision that you have to do it with a whole heart.

Dan: In the wake of two disastrous marriages when I was younger, I felt like a relationship failure. After dating Ariel for a few years, she began to pressure me to get married and called me a commitment-phobe when I resisted. I felt like I needed to prove to her, myself, and my family and friends that I could make and keep a commitment. Later I realized that was a pretty lame reason to marry; that relationship did not last much longer than the previous ones.

Donna: While I was dating Terry, my mother became ill and passed away. Terry was very kind and supportive to me during that trying time. Soon afterward he proposed to me. At the time I was emotionally tender, and I felt indebted to him for all his care, so I said yes. Five years and two children later, Terry grew terribly demanding and our marriage became a battle-field. In retrospect I recognized that I should not have let a sense of "owingness" guide my marriage decision.

Stacy: When I met Brad, I knew there was greatness in him. He had some problems, but I felt that with enough love and belief I could help him turn his life around and become the man I envisioned. When we got married, though, things just got worse. He still did not hold a job, and he spent his evenings watching TV and smoking pot. After three years of my loving efforts, he was no better off and neither was I. I did not marry a man—I married his potential.

Greg: Gina and I lived together for two years, and she moved out when I told her I didn't think I felt enough to go the distance with her. A month later she told me that she was starting to see someone else. I was afraid I would lose her, so I proposed to her. During our marriage we hit the same wall. We both learned that fear of losing makes a faulty foundation for a relationship.

TOP 10 REASONS NOT TO GET MARRIED

1. *To have your dream wedding.*

A wedding is not a goal in itself, but a natural expression of the joining that already exists. Bridezilla confuses the *symbol* of a relationship with the relationship itself. A wedding is an event; a marriage is a state of mind and heart. If you are not already married in your heart, your Cinderella wedding's twenty-one-gun salute is firing blanks.

Some people are more wedding-happy than they are happy. My friends Stan and Leslie had no fewer than six wedding ceremonies. Over a period of several months the couple stood before a rabbi, priest, Native American medicine man, Hawaiian kahuna, Mexican shaman, and a yogi to unite them in holy matrimony. Six months later I saw Stan at a party by himself. "Where's Leslie?" I had to ask.

"Oh, we broke up," he explained.

Moral of the story: All the weddings in the world can't make a marriage stick if you don't.

Create a real marriage in your hearts, keep your priorities straight, and your wedding will be the happiest and most holy event on the planet. Consider:

Am I more interested in my wedding, or my marriage?

2. *You are flattered by the proposal, or your partner is pressuring you.*

Enthusiasm is the key success factor in all endeavors. Marriage, which may be your most important life decision, should sparkle with true choice and be an action, not a reaction. If it's not a "Hell, yes!" it's a "Hell, no!"

INSECURE PEOPLE:	SECURE PEOPLE:
Follow external voices	Follow internal choices
Are motivated by fear	Are motivated by joy
Act adaptively	Act creatively
Are ruled by ego	Are ruled by spirit
Override their feelings	Trust their feelings
Are satisfied with a lukewarm relationship	Require passion

Healthy decisions light you up; unhealthy decisions prop you up. Is your delight overwhelming or underwhelming? If your friends comment, "Wow, you're really glowing—what have you been up to?" you know you are on the right track. If any of them ask you if you have given your marriage sufficient forethought, do consider their question.

Just because someone wants you does not mean you want them. Sure, it is a compliment to be loved and desired, but love and desire must flow in both directions for a marriage to work. Give your partner the gift of your full choice, or your honesty otherwise. There is someone out there you would really want to be with. If he or she is standing in front of you, dive with open arms. If not, step away from the diving board.

Is this wedding my choice or one that is being imposed on me?

3. *You want to prove you can make a commitment or settle down.*
People on a mission to prove something to the world set themselves up to lose before they begin. Two flaws in reasoning can sabotage even apparently noble efforts: (1) they believe there is something wrong with them that they need to rectify and show the world they have achieved, and (2) they give the opinions of others undue power and act on them.

Marrying to prove yourself is a slippery varmint to identify and remedy, because hardly anyone who does so is aware of their purpose at the time. No one I know has ever proposed thus: "Sonia, I am ashamed of my past history of unfulfilled relationships, so I would like you to be my wife and help me show the people who have judged me that I am capable of making and keeping a commitment." *Exit Sonia, stage left.* If the proposer were more self-aware, he would rethink his proposal. But most of the programming that undermines our joy lies just below the surface of our awareness, and we rarely face it until we are sitting across the table from someone we thought we loved, this time with lawyers between us. This need not be.

People who love and believe in you do not need to be convinced, and people who do not love or believe in you are not worth trying to convince. Before heading for the altar, consider what you would do if no one else were watching. If you are using your union as a personal, social, or political statement, your mixed agenda will come back to bite you in the butt, and you will ultimately have to tell the truth about what your true decision would have been if you did not have something to broadcast.

If you feel you need to prove something through a relationship, consider:

- *What would I be doing if social opinion were not a factor in my decision?*
- *Who in my life do I feel I need to prove myself to? Is their voice in my head still calling the shots?*
- *If I knew I was okay as I am, how would I proceed?*

You do not need to prove anything to anyone. Real relationships speak for themselves and don't need you or anyone to advertise them. The more you try to convince others of something, the more you are trying to convince yourself. Once again we arrive at the all-important touchstone of authenticity, which will net you a lot more mileage than spin.

4. *You feel like you owe it to your partner.*
Kindness is holy and must never be overlooked. Yet obligation is not a valid reason for a relationship or marriage. If you are going to invest your life to be with a partner, you must burn with the fire of purpose. You must be moved from the depths of your soul, not a sense of duty.

If you feel obligated to have a relationship, sleep with, or marry someone because you owe him something, or he is trying to guilt you into a commitment, ask yourself, "What would I be doing if I didn't feel a sense of debt?" Would you value his intimate company for who he is? Has he helped you because he loves you and wants to support you, or because he wants something from you? Has he attached strings to his gift? Have you?

In many cultures marriages have been politically, socially, economically, or religiously driven, like business deals. While romantic love has its pitfalls, it at least honors the choice of the heart over externally dictated duty. Your duty to your spirit far exceeds your duty to a guilt bargain. Say yes because of love, or do not say it at all.

5. *You intend to help your partner realize his true potential.*
It is said, "A woman marries a man with the expectation he will

change, and a man marries a woman with the expectation she will never change." I cannot count the number of women in my seminars who, after having been married for five, ten, or twenty years, wistfully report, "When I married my husband, he had a (drinking) (overworking) (cheating) problem, but I knew that with enough love I could transform him." Yet in most cases the undesirable behavior did not get better, but worse.

Falling in love with someone's potential is more of an issue for women than for men. Over many years counseling thousands of clients, I have never heard one man say, "I married her because I saw something great in her that I knew that with enough love and belief I could bring forth and help her realize her true potential." What I have heard is, "She really turned my head when she walked into the room," or, "I could be myself with her."

The answer to misappropriated hope is not damp cynicism or reinforced optimism, but a healthy balance between lofty vision and current reality. Here is a crucial question:

If my partner never changed one bit from the way he is today, would I be happy to spend my life with him?

If your answer is yes, you have a good grip on who you are getting involved with, and you are setting up your relationship to win. If, five months or five years down the road, you would be pissed off if he still didn't come home by 6:00 PM, your vision may be clouded by your unspoken agenda. Love the person for who he is, or don't claim that you love him.

Getting other people to change, especially in an intimate relationship, is a paradox. The more you try to fix someone, the more resistant they become (like, uh, guys). The more you love them as they are, the more likely they are to step into their innate strength. When you celebrate your partner's valuable qualities, you draw them forth. When you harp on what is not working, those traits will intensify. True greatness grows not though demand, but through acceptance and appreciation.

6. *You marry your partner to avoid losing her.*
Stuart Emery noted, "Most relationships are based on fear of losing." People in a fear or survival mentality do all kinds of unhealthy things that someone who trusted him- or herself (and the process of relationship) would not do. Although it is important to appreciate your partner and recognize the value she brings to your life, it is an unwise move to put a ring on her finger because you are afraid she will go away if you don't.
  Your question:

If I know I am safe and I have the right and power to attract and sustain a relationship with a partner who would stay with me, what current behaviors would I drop? What actions would I replace them with?

PARTNERS WHO ACT FROM FEAR OF LOSS:	PARTNERS WHO ACT WITH CONFIDENCE:
Do not disclose true feelings	Share honest feelings
Avoid confronting their partner	Confront their partner when necessary

Withhold expressions of love	Express their love freely
Manipulate with guilt	Support their partner to be him- or herself
Make ostentatious public displays of love and affection	Express love intimately and appropriately
Hustle to please their partner at the expense of joy	Balance pleasing their partner with pleasing their self
Make rash proposals	Propose when they are ready and sure

You cannot lose someone or something that belongs to you by virtue of a strong and loving connection. When you act because you are afraid of losing, you end up losing. Tap in to your true deservingness and recognize your worth to sustain a great relationship, and you will not have to struggle to keep what you already own.

7. *You hope marriage will glue a relationship that hasn't stuck so far.* Two maxims guide here:

> *Struggle to get, struggle to keep.*
> *A rocky road to marriage does not end at the altar.*

A wedding may symbolize hope on the part of one or both partners that this relationship will work out. But if it's not working out before the wedding, it will probably not work out after the wedding. A good relationship stands on its own merit and does not require a wedding to save it. A house does not make a home, a job does not make a livelihood, and a wedding does not make a marriage. People make a marriage, and what you make of it reveals itself right where you stand.

If you are depending on your wedding to salvage an ailing relationship, face and handle your issues now. Some possible routes you might take:

- Be honest with each other about your feelings, desires, intentions, and reservations about the marriage.
- See a counselor or therapist together to help you clarify your intentions for marriage.
- Ask people you respect if they see your relationship as ready for marriage.
- Postpone the wedding until you feel like you are on solid ground.

Running the gantlet of these processes may ultimately send you in opposite directions, but it might also deliver strength and readiness. Many people ascribe magical beliefs to marriage in order to avoid dealing with the issues they are facing at the moment. Yet it is the very handling of these issues that will solidify their platform for marriage.

If my relationship didn't get any better after our wedding, would I go through with it?

8. *Show off your trophy (bride) (husband) to friends and family.*
You win the booby prize, but lose the game of love. Litmus test:

Would I be with him if no one else ever saw me with him?

Pick someone who pleases you for who he is, not how he shows.
    Variation on this theme: *Marry into money, move into nice house, and swim in a disappearing-edge pool.* Watch what else disappears. Nice stuff is fun, but should be regarded as an afterthought. *Am I in love with the picture or the frame?* Substance should come first, and the icing, second.

9. *This partner is everything your last partner wasn't.*
Husband number one was irresponsible; new hubby always follows through. Last wife was overbearing; new wife is soft and agreeable. There are many variations on these themes. Is your marriage an action, or a reaction? Are you satisfying yourself, or simply flipping the bird at the last goon? If your new partner embodies attractive traits your ex missed, do they lack some traits your ex embodied? If you never had that marriage or relationship, would you be so attracted to this new partner? Do your best to clear your palate and evaluate your partner on his or her own merits, as if you were starting from scratch.

Am I seeing my partner clearly, or as a reaction to my history?

10. *You have a hidden agenda:*
Often hidden agendas are hidden even from the one holding them. Considering these possibilities may bring one or more to light:

- You want to prove you are attractive and desirable.
- Your partner is your (mentor) (therapist) (guru) (boss), and you hope he or she will (guide) (heal) (enlighten) (professionally advance) you.
- Marrying will get your parents off your back.
- Marrying will annoy the hell out of your parents, who don't approve of your lifestyle or partner.
- A hetero marriage will prove you are straight (when you're not).
- You are aching to have a child, and this partner can help.
- You love the hot sex (only).

Your question:

Do I have an agenda for marriage other than a sincere desire to be with my partner?

People get married for all kinds of reasons they regret. In the next chapter we will look at reasons that work. If you can learn from the examples here and save yourself and your partner pain and tears, this chapter is well worth it. And so are you.

WHAT YOU CAN DO ABOUT IT, POINT BY POINT

- Ask yourself why you want to get married—and answer honestly.
- When choosing a spouse, discern between accoutrements and substance.
- Never marry for flattery, pressure, or debt.

- Evaluate your partner on the basis of who he is now, not his potential.
- If you believe that marriage will solidify an ailing relationship, face and handle your issues before you go to the altar.
- Do not let fear of loss dictate your actions. Tap in to your confidence and proceed from strength.

How to Know Who to Marry

—⁂—

Dr. Norman Vincent Peale was sitting on an airplane next to a young woman who struck up a conversation with him. When she discovered that Dr. Peale was a man of seasoned wisdom, she decided to ask him for help with a dilemma. "I have been dating two men, and both of them have proposed to me," she explained. "I'm not sure which one to say 'yes' to. Can you give me some advice?"

"Sure," Dr. Peale answered abruptly. "I don't think you should marry either of them."

"Why is that?" asked the young lady, surprised.

"If you have to ask me who to marry, you're not in love with either of them," he answered.

TOP 10 REASONS TO GET MARRIED

1. You love your partner and want to be with her.
2. You already feel married in your heart, and a ceremony would symbolize your connection.
3. The chemistry of being together generates more joy and aliveness than you experience individually.
4. You feel at home, relaxed, safe, and free to be yourself in your partner's presence.
5. You share common interests, values, and visions, and you communicate well intellectually and emotionally.
6. You support each other to achieve your personal goals and visions.
7. Your sexual connection brings you closer to your partner and yourself.
8. The quantity of your joyful time together far exceeds the quantity of upset.
9. Your life works better and you generate more success with your partner in it.
10. You feel that life has sent you this person as a blessing and gift of love.

Since love is natural and rewarding relationships are our birthright, the reasons for a healthy marriage are far simpler and more obvious than the convoluted reasons that would contraindicate it. When someone asked Dr. Peale why he was still married to his wife after more than fifty years together, he answered simply, "I feel very happy in her presence." There may not be much more to it than that.

The heart has reasons that reason knows not. If you love

and care about your partner and want to be with her, no other reason is necessary; if you don't love her or really want to be with her, no reason is enough.

How do you know if you are supposed to marry a particular person? Ask yourself what is the most dominant feeling in your heart and gut about it. When you think about being with this person, do you feel lifted and enthusiastic? Does the idea bring you life? Would you be sad if you were not with him? Try not to think about it too hard. If there are obvious reasons not to marry, heed them. Otherwise, look inside yourself for the answer. You already know. Tell the truth about your feelings, and decisions will make themselves.

If you are not sure, don't marry. Don't make believe you know when you don't. Instead, wait and watch. You will either know that you want to marry this person, or that you don't. If you are having trouble getting in touch with your guidance, say a prayer or make a request of the universe:

> *"Please show me if this person is right for me.*
> *Let me know deeply from inside out.*
> *I am willing to know."*

I assure you that if you pray or ask sincerely, you will know. You just will.

Many of my clients have reported that when they met their partner, something inside them knew deeply that they were to be with this person, and there was no doubt in their mind. They dove in and had glowing results. Others reported that when they received a proposal, something inside them knew they would regret it if they said yes. Some of these people heeded their inner warning and were glad they did. Others did not heed it and spent years in a loveless marriage. Yet all of them learned the importance of consulting their inner knowing and trusting it.

IF YOU DON'T KNOW INSTANTLY

Sometimes love takes time to brew. If you meet someone and do not get an immediate inner "yes," this doesn't mean you are not suited for each other; it just means that you do not know instantly. You may discover more of your true feelings over time. Sometimes love that grows gradually over time is more real and powerful than love that hits you over the head. Both can work; you just have to be honest about what you feel.

You may have doubts or fears before committing; many, maybe most, people do. The question is: how large do your doubts or fears loom in contrast to your enthusiasm? Are you mostly sure and excited, and a little worried? Or are you mostly hesitant and little excited? I would move ahead only if my excitement significantly outweighed my resistance. If you are mostly afraid or leery, either (1) you are receiving inner guidance that this step is not right for you; or (2) the relationship may be a good one, but your fears will likely sabotage your potential joy. In either case, you must come to terms with your hesitation and either honor it or grow beyond it. Put your thoughts and feelings honestly on the table before you with your partner, trusted, friends, or a counselor, and they will reveal the truth behind them.

Either you know, or you don't know. If you know, act. If you don't know, wait. Trust your gut.

WHAT YOU CAN DO ABOUT IT, POINT BY POINT

- When considering marriage, consult and trust the deepest knowing of your heart rather than your head.
- If in doubt, don't. Wait, watch, and pray, or ask for signs of guidance.
- If your enthusiasm is far greater than your doubts, move ahead.
- Sometimes love does not reveal itself at first sight, but grows over time. Be open to this process.

YOU DON'T END RELATIONSHIPS CLEANLY.

It's a lot easier to start a relationship than to end one. Yet how you end a relationship shows more about your character than how you start one, and can actually deepen your relationship with your partner even though you are parting. Many people, out of fear, upset, or lack of skill, end relationships in unconscious or unkind ways. Relationship-ending skills can be a huge asset to you and your partner and leave you with a sense of integrity rather than bitterness. Most important, skillful endings leave you in the perfect position to meet someone with whom you can have your heart's desire.

WHAT YOU CAN DO ABOUT IT

The following chapters will show you how to:
- Be honest and direct with your partner rather than leaving in an indirect way.
- Recognize if your partner is trying to leave you without saying so openly.
- Decide if, when, or how to see each other again.
- End relationships cleanly so that you are open and available to a better relationship with someone new.

You Can't Fire Me—I Quit

When Hal was ten years old, he had a "girlfriend" named Carolyn. When Carolyn came to visit her dad in Hal's neighborhood on weekends, the two would pal around. Carolyn was sweet and Hal liked her a lot.

On Friday nights a mobile pizza truck would park itself in the neighborhood and folks would line up to order pizza. One night while standing behind Carolyn in line, as a joke Hal kept tossing a football at her. She didn't like it and protested. But Hal kept doing it, to the point that he hurt her. Carolyn got angry and pushed him away. That was the end of their "romance."

Years later, after going through many painful relationships, Hal realized that night with Carolyn was a foreshadowing of a self-defeating pattern to follow: Hal would push women away before they could leave him. He "made" them leave before he would get hurt, but still lost out on what he really wanted.

The list of ways we hurt ourselves in relationships is long and heartbreaking. One of those ways is to avoid rejection by leaving first. This makes no sense, since you end up with the result you were trying to avoid—a lost relationship. Yet according to fear's twisted reasoning, quitting offers a buffer from pain. How sad that we hurt ourselves doing things to keep from being hurt.

If you have a pattern of leaving your partners before they leave you, here are some steps to correct it:

1. *Recognize and own the pattern.* Many daters continuously find fault with their partners and never consider that they are generating their breakups. If you keep leaving people, the pattern has less to do with your dates and more to do with you. You may have many reasons and excuses why your relationships tank, yet none are as powerful as admitting that you prefer to bail before you get dumped.

2. *Identify the fears that make bailing more attractive than staying.* Is it too scary to face being rejected? Does the idea of intimacy overwhelm you? Have you been left before, and you still bear the wounds? Does leaving first give you a sense of power and control? Are you worried that you might get trapped in a distasteful situation?

3. *Acknowledge that leaving before you are left is not getting you what you really want.* Breaking things off first might buy you a momentary sense of safety, but you

are missing out on intimacy, mutual support, friendship, companionship, great sex, cutting-edge
growth, and perhaps a lifelong connection—not a
wise tradeoff. Even a little contemplation will reveal
that there is much more out there than you have
been settling for. Set change in motion by focusing
on what you can have instead of what you have been
accepting.

4. *Use your next relationship to practice shifting the pattern.* Your moment of opportunity comes when you
get into a new relationship and you are tempted to
jump ship. Instead of finding an excuse to leave,
communicate with your partner. Tell him or her,
"This is getting kind of scary to me. I have left other
relationships at this point, but I don't want to keep
doing that. I want to create a relationship that
works." That simple statement may be enough to
jettison you out of the orbit of your old pattern. If
you are dating someone who respects sincerity, he
will feel closer to you and likely open up more to
you, creating a safe foundation for both of you. If he
runs away, don't worry; you will have plenty more
opportunities to practice. Intention is the key, and it
always gets results sooner or later.

THE BALL IS IN YOUR COURT

Self-demolition is at the root of more breakups than most
people recognize. If you quit to avoid being fired, you are still

out of a job. And if you were not going to be fired, you are *really* out of a job. While you may believe that partners are doing it to you, you are the only one who can destroy or redeem your love life. It matters not how long you have been on the run or how badly you have botched things. The moment you wake up, or are even willing to wake up, you open the door to more rewarding results. When you refuse to run from your good, it will find you right where you stand.

WHAT YOU CAN DO ABOUT IT, POINT BY POINT

- Recognize and accept your role in ending relationships before you get dumped.
- Identify and admit the fears that move you to split.
- Acknowledge that bailing, while offering you momentary safety, is keeping you from the intimacy you desire.
- Consider how great a relationship could be if both partners continually showed up to be with each other.
- When tempted to bail, communicate your fears and feelings rather than vacating.

I Forgot to Tell You
We Broke Up

—∾∾—

Dennis had an unusual method of breaking up with his girl-friends: He would sleep with his girlfriend's best friend. When his girlfriend found out (she always did), she would grow furious and leave the relationship, saving Dennis the trouble of being the one who left.

Though Dennis's pattern doesn't say a lot for his character (or that of his girlfriends' friends), it does illustrate how some people end relationships indirectly when they can't find the courage to be upfront.

The old song lyric "Breakin' up is hard to do" is sometimes truer for the partner who is leaving than the one who is left. Let's face it: it's never fun to dismiss someone you've been involved with. Some people would avoid such confrontation at all costs and find roundabout ways to leave rather than having to look a lover in the eye and say good-bye.

If you have trouble ending relationships, these tips will make it easier when that difficult moment comes:

- Most people appreciate honesty more than deception, manipulation, game playing, or nonaction.
- Most people would rather hear the truth from you directly rather than find it out from a third party.
- Clean breaks, while initially painful, help both partners in the long run. Ripping off a Band-Aid hurts, but not as much as slowly pulling off your arm hairs one by one.
- Your partner probably already senses that you have left emotionally, so why make believe you are there when you are not?
- When you let go of a relationship that is not working for you, you free yourself and your partner to find a better one.

SIGNS

If you sense that your partner has broken up with you without telling you, here are some signs you may be right. He or she:

- Doesn't respond to your phone calls or e-mails.
- Sends you a long, complicated e-mail with lots of rationales and metaphors, expecting you to read between the lines.
- Is too busy or doesn't feel well enough to get together.
- Just doesn't feel like having sex anymore.
- Says and does obnoxious things that hurt you.

- Creates a huge fight so that you think it was something you did, or that it was the fight that broke you up.
- Starts dating (or sleeping with) someone else, and you hear about it from a third party.
- Tells you he or she needs space, and you hardly hear from your partner again.

THE CURE

The cure for innuendo and circuitousness is honest, direct communication. If your partner is not communicating, invite her to do so by being completely honest yourself. Tell her what you are seeing and sensing, and ask her what's going on inside her. Ask her directly how she is feeling about being together. At this point your conversation and relationship may take one of several directions. Your partner:

1. Has no response. (*Shoulder shrug.*)
2. Denies there is anything is wrong. (*"Everything's cool, baby."*)
3. Splits. (*"Gotta go, the game's starting."*)
4. Shifts blame. (*"What, are you paranoid or something? How come you have to analyze everything?"*)
5. Tries to distract you. (*"Come on, sugar, let's have some lovin'."*)
6. Tells the truth. (*"Well, I have been thinking about our relationship, and . . ."*)

Many people would still prefer responses 1 to 5 rather than 6, because 6 is, well, scary. You might hear something you don't want to hear, and the relationship might end. So you keep your mouth shut, grab a joint, hop into bed, or turn on Letterman, and the painful cycle just goes on. But eventually you will both have to speak your truth. Wisdom calls you to make that day be sooner rather than later.

NOW FOR THE GOOD NEWS

Sometimes "Well, I have been thinking about our relationship" leads not to the end of the relationship, but the beginning. Instead of that sentence ending with "and I don't think it's working out," it ends with, "and I have strong feelings for you that I don't know what to do with"; or "we're getting so close that I get scared and shut down"; or "I got pissed off when you were talking to your former boyfriend"; or some other statement that leads to deeper communication and richer connection. Often you don't know until you ask. Yet one thing is for sure: honesty will get you a lot more mileage than hiding.

There's no getting around it: relationships are a lot more fun to start than to end. But endings are not necessarily bad; often they pave a way to something better with that partner or a new one. *How* you end is more important than *that* you end. Artful endings bring people together in ways that never would have happened if you did it less skillfully. Some people grow closer through breaking up than they ever grew in their relationship. At least you will respect yourself, and your partner will not feel burned, but valued. So we've come full circle to our earlier lesson on starting relationships with realness. That's how you end them, too.

*Great is the art of beginning. Even
greater is the art of ending.*
—*Longfellow*

WHAT YOU CAN DO ABOUT IT, POINT BY POINT

- If you must end a relationship, do so with honesty, directness, and kindness.
- Clean breaks are more helpful to both partners than vague or wishy-washy ones.
- Pay attention to the signs (listed above) that your partner may be disappearing without telling you.
- Ask your partner directly what he is feeling about being with you, and be open to his response.
- Odd though it may sound, seek to use your breakup to grow closer to each other.

From Clean Endings
to New Beginnings

—◦◦◦—

On a blind date Ryan met Leslie, described to him by a mutual friend as an attractive, intelligent, and openhearted woman. After spending a little time with Leslie, he found that she was all of that, and more.

Ryan and Leslie dated for several months, and he liked her a lot. Yet he did not feel strongly enough about her to create the committed relationship she wanted. The two continued to see each other, but their time together was lackluster.

Finally Leslie confronted Ryan and told him that she needed to know if he was in the relationship or out; for her there was no middle ground. After giving her question some serious thought, Ryan realized he was out, and told her.

"Thank you," Leslie replied. "That's what I needed to know." The two ended their goopy conversation and relationship on a friendly note, and Ryan did not hear from Leslie again.

This book is all about helping you shift from unfulfilling dates and relationships to alive, energized, rewarding connections. One of the strongest moves you can make on your own behalf is to skillfully cut the cord of relationships that aren't headed where you choose to go. Think of your love life as a DVD. You have just so much space on your disk—time, energy, presence, and emotions—for a relationship. If much or most of your disk is filled with people and activities that don't work for you, you have little capacity to receive new and better ones. At some point you need to erase from your disk what is blocking love so that you can open the door to receive it. Our final chapter will help you refine those all-important skills.

In the example above, Leslie bestowed Ryan with a real gift: she made a clean break. Once she knew Ryan was not going any further with her, she was out of there. She wasn't angry, and she didn't begrudge their time together. She just didn't want to stay on a train not going to her destination.

If you have difficulty ending relationships, it might be because of one of these reasons:

- You feel too guilty to say good-bye.
- You are afraid you might be making the wrong choice.
- You believe you may have a good thing in spite of your doubts or upsets.
- You fear you may not be able to do any better.
- It's more convenient to stay than to trudge through the upset caused by leaving.
- The relationship offers you "gifts" that you are reluctant to let go of—for example, material comforts; having power over your partner; looking cool as a couple; etc.

- You and/or your partner do not have great communication skills, and putting your cards on the table is difficult for one or both of you.
- You believe that relationships are supposed to be difficult, so why bother trying to find a good one?

WACKY THINGS PEOPLE DO TO KEEP THE DRAMA GOING

In spite of good reasons to part, I have seen (and done) all kinds of things that keep relationships in force after partners have decided to break up:

- Have sex one more time.
- Decide to stay friends and have sex once in a while.
- Have one more conversation about your feelings about breaking up.
- Get together because you feel lonely or don't want to sit home on a Saturday night.
- Send him or her a gift.
- Call him or her for counseling about your new relationship.
- Get pregnant together.
- Create an emergency that forces you to get together to handle it.
- Start a business or buy property together.
- Keep tabs on him or her to find out if he or she is seeing someone new.
- Flaunt your new relationship to your former partner.
- Badmouth your former partner to common friends.

- Long for the good times you had while forgetting why you parted.

SMART THINGS PEOPLE DO TO GET FREE AND GET A LIFE

If you are ready to get on with your life and make space for a relationship that works, these tips will help you:

- Say good-bye with clarity, surety, and respect.
- Don't initiate or encourage contact with your former partner. If necessary, don't respond to his or her attempts to contact you.
- Don't sleep with him or her.
- Remember why you left the relationship.
- Send your former partner good thoughts and appreciation from a distance.
- Take time to be with yourself, get to know who you are at this point, and enjoy your own company.
- Consider any unhealthy reasons you were drawn to or stayed with your former partner, and be sensitive to thoughts or actions that may re-create that.
- Do things outside of relationship—with yourself or friends—for pure joy and self-nurturing.

---

*Keep your eyes on the road ahead
and look in the rearview mirror only
to avoid accidents.*
—Dan McKinnon

CAN YOU BE FRIENDS AFTER BEING LOVERS?

Certainly. Usually, however, you need a clearing-out period during which you and/or your partner take time to step back, reconnect with yourself, contemplate what you learned, and set a new course. The length of this period is unique to you and your relationship, so tune in to your needs. Do you really want to remain friends? If not, don't go through the motions. If you still value your former partner and want him to be a part of your life, that is a tender but masterful path, and you can have it if you like. Just be sensitive to its right timing. (My earlier book *Happily Even After* deals with this process exclusively and in great detail, should you want to pursue a post-breakup friendship.)

Indecision in ending relationships, like all aspects of life, is debilitating; choice is empowering. Indecision usually stems from fear; choice, from trust and confidence. Indecision usually keeps an unrewarding status quo in force; choice makes way for new and better. If you are having a hard time ending a relationship that you feel is not in your best interests, or you have ended one and you are in an uncomfortable zone between relationships or anxious about being alone, remember this: you are on a journey to find and have what you really want. Although part of you believes that relationships are painful, part of you knows they can be deeply rewarding. Do not stop until you find the reward you seek. No matter how disappointing your recent breakup or how many disasters you have weathered, the story is not over. There is a partner for you, and you have great gifts to offer a partner. When wisely bidding a former partner good-bye, or being on the receiving end of a good-bye, the door is opening for better. In spite of temporary sorrows or setbacks, life keeps going from good to better, and your world of relationship will keep expanding as you allow love to have its way.

WHAT YOU CAN DO ABOUT IT, POINT BY POINT

- If you are ending a relationship, end it cleanly, clearly, and consciously.
- Don't keep having sex or create dramas as excuses to stay intertwined. Minimize or eliminate contact if necessary.
- Shift your vision to where you now stand and what is next.
- If at some point you wish to get together again, do so only if both of you have changed.

Afterword

————

TOWARD THE END OF his Hawaiian vacation, my friend Jack came to visit me. As I drove Jack to the airport, he confessed, "There were two things I always dreamed of doing with my beloved, and waited to do with her when she came along. One was to buy a house in a neighborhood I have always loved, and the other was to visit Hawaii. Last year I decided to quit waiting for my beloved to show up before I could enjoy those gifts. I bought the house, and now I have come to Hawaii and had a stellar vacation." Jack went on, "Now I realize that I have done those things with my beloved. My beloved, you see, is me."

When I next saw Jack, he introduced me to his fiancée. When he found his beloved inside him, he found his beloved beside him.

Over years of counseling people in pain and despair about their relationships (including myself), I have been inspired to observe many happy endings. This has taught me that no dating difficulty is so overwhelming that you cannot find your way home; indeed, some of the most painful predicaments are preludes to glorious triumph.

Take Hannah, for example, a young Jewish woman who fell in love with a Muslim man. Hannah's father was furious about his daughter's romance and forbade her to date Rashid. Over several years Hannah attended my seminars and plodded through the saga of her star-crossed love. Finally she mailed me a copy of a letter she wrote to her father explaining to him that she appreciated all he had done for her—but this was her life and this was the man she loved, and she could no longer deny her heart's calling. A year later I received Hannah's wedding picture, and the following year her baby's photo. Eventually her father dropped his resistance and accepted Rashid into his heart and family.

Then there was Erin, the wedding coordinator who could get everyone to the altar but herself. When she finally admitted that she was in the wedding business because she really wanted to be in a wedding, she let a good man into her life. Then someone else planned the wedding at which she finally walked down the aisle herself.

All dating, of course, does not have to lead to marriage. It can lead to great dates and a deeper relationship with yourself. Bill was something of a Shallow Hal, regularly tossing women aside the moment he found the tiniest flaw in them. After a painful breakup Bill realized that he did not like women because he did not like himself. His father had demanded perfection of him, which he could not live up to, so he projected his sense of frailty onto women and judged them for all of his own failings. When he recognized his pattern, he lightened up on both himself and his dates, and began to create relationships that worked.

You, too, can have dates and relationships that work, but first you must fall in love with yourself. Or at least like yourself more. Or at least give yourself a break from the harsh judgments that obscured your vision of all the good you can offer and receive. Or find worthiness in yourself to let someone wonderful in. So we end our book, and perhaps a chapter of your life, on a note of confident encouragement: when you find the love inside you that you sought in an outer lover, you will have both.

Acknowledgments

———

THIS BOOK IS A result of everything I have learned about relationships, sometimes through joy and sometimes through pain. Yet every moment has served, and I stand in awe at the perfection of the journey, and gratitude to everyone who has contributed to it.

I honor my beloved partner, Dee, whom I regard as the prize at the end of the road of my seeking. I feel blessed to walk side by side with a woman of such extraordinary strength, wisdom, and love.

I honor the women I have dated and with whom I have shared relationships, who have been among the most important teachers in my life. Some have taught me through intimacy and others have taught me through challenge. Yet all experiences have served and assisted me to grow to arrive at the place I now stand.

I acknowledge my male friends who celebrated the good times with me and supported me during stressful times. Brotherhood is holy.

I honor myself for the fortitude to persevere; for choosing compassion for myself and others when judgment ranted; for the love I have expressed; and for being willing to use all my experiences for growth.

I am deeply grateful to Kathy McDuff for her tireless support of this work and taking immaculate care of clients and colleagues; and to her husband Rich Lucas for his quiet yet consistent support of our mission to serve.

Thank you to Michael Ebeling and Kristina Holmes for joining the manuscript with the perfect publisher for it.

Much appreciation and respect for my editor Renée Sedliar, who recognized the importance of our message and took the time and caring to go through the material with a fine-tooth comb and offer her expertise to groom it to its most powerful expression.

And to you, the reader, a friend whom I may never meet in person, but whose life has intersected mine in a domain that is crucial to both of our hearts. May your life be better for our meeting.

Learn More with Alan Cohen

—⁓—

IF YOU HAVE ENJOYED and found value in *Don't Get Lucky—Get Smart*, you are invited to explore Alan Cohen's in-person or online seminars:

> *Daily Inspirational Quotes and Monthly E-Newsletter:* Receive an uplifting quote daily via e-mail and Alan's monthly newsletter containing inspiring stories, recommendations, and updates on Alan's latest events, new books, and other offerings.

> *Online Courses:* Receive a lesson each day via e-mail for one month, and participate in a teleseminar (class via telephone). Subjects include: "Building Great Relationships," "Relax into Wealth," "The Time of Your Life," and "Handle with Prayer."

The Life Mastery Training: A six-day residential retreat at an inspiring location, to reconnect with yourself, tap in to your passion, clarify your next step, and receive support from Alan and a group of peers. Currently offered in Sedona, Maui, and Fiji.

Personal Mentorship: Study closely with Alan and receive direct personal guidance to make powerful life choices. Monthly personal coaching, small group retreat, and a committed connection between you, Alan, and like-minded people to enable you to shine in every aspect of your life and become all you can be.

To register or receive more information on the above:

Visit: www.alancohen.com
E-mail: info@alancohen.com
Phone: (800) 568-3079
(808) 572-0001 (outside U.S.)
Fax: (808) 572-1023

or write to:

Alan Cohen Publications
P.O. Box 835
Haiku, Hawaii 96708, U.S.A.